The American
BUTLER

Other publications available from the author on Amazon.com

"Front of the House: What Every Chef Must Know"

"Restaurant: The Owner's Manual –
A Guide to Staff Training for Owners and Management"

"Waiter International"

Works on the Web:

Now available:

www.StopSmokingPDQ
With Larry O. Knight, CCDC
Certified Chemical Dependent Counselor
Mission College, Los Angeles

Work in progress:
www.TheSportsMind/BodyConnection
With Larry O. Knight, CMT
Certified Meditation Teacher, The Chopra Institute

For more details, please email: larryorenknight825@gmail.com

The American BUTLER

AN EDUCATIONAL AND INFORMATIONAL MEMOIR

BY

LARRY O. KNIGHT, MASTER BUTLER

iUniverse, Inc.
Bloomington

THE AMERICAN BUTLER
An Educational and Informational Memoir

iUniverse books may be ordered through booksellers or by contacting:

iUniverse
1663 Liberty Drive
Bloomington, IN 47403
www.iuniverse.com
1-800-Authors (1-800-288-4677)

ISBN: 978-1-4620-6935-4 (sc)
ISBN: 978-1-4620-6936-1 (ebk)

Printed in the United States of America

iUniverse rev. date: 11/19/2011

Dedication

To those kind, beautiful, talented ladies

Ms. Carol Burnett

Mrs. Barbara Davis

Ms. Candace Bergen

World Class, First Class

Acknowledgement

Thank you, Jackie Hendrickson—I could not have done this without you.

And to my very good friend, John Murphy—
None of this would have come to pass without your kind encouragement and genuine love.

"Let me tell you about the very rich. They are different from you and me."

F. Scott Fitzgerald

So, you want to be a Butler?

So, you're thinking about hiring a Butler?

So you just want to know about butler service in America?

If none of the above, buy the book anyway. It's great fun.

This book is the real deal.

No phony accents, no phony uniforms and no B.S.

Real stories, real people and real, useable, information.

I hereby pass on to you my experience, strengths, weaknesses,
enthusiasm and joy for a
profession I loved then and love now.

Enjoy,

Larry O. Knight, Master Butler

Famous New York City Restaurateur reminds his staff each night, "Tonight, it is a
Ballet and not a Rodeo." (Agnes De Mille not withstanding.)

Table of Contents

Special Supplement:

"Waiter International"
The Ultimate and Complete Guide
To Becoming a Truly Professional Waiter

Section I

THE BUTLER BUSINESS

Forget everything you've seen in the movies or read in a book. The American Butler comes in two models—Private and Public (hotels, casinos, etc.)

In the Private Sector, especially in the West, you may find want ads seeking Butler/Cook, Butler/Houseman, and Butler/Valet, (that's pronounced Valet. A valet, pronounced vala', parks your car) or the Granddaddy of them all, Butler/Cook/Houseman/Valet/—this final space is reserved for the word "Slave." Beware of anything that has a slash, especially two or more!

If you have limited experience in the service world, you might want to consider "Houseman" or "Houseman/Cook" if, in fact, you can cook and know how to run a vacuum and make a bed properly. Look for the smaller ads—for Driver, Assistant, etc.

Two of the best jobs I ever had came from just this sort of ad. In most large cities there are Domestic Agencies. They will work with you if you have the right attitude and a decent look, even if you have little or no experience.

My first job came from a small ad seeking a live-in houseman. My last job was as a property manager.

I acquired the title of Major Domo, by applying for an ad that said "Driver" and little else. My last butler job was Senior Butler, The Bellagio, Las Vegas. It was a long, long trip from the first position to the last one—a period of thirty years.

Most hotels and casinos hire within. If your goal is to be a butler, you may want to find a hotel, resort etc., which offers butler service. Get in the door, even if it's as a bus person, waiter or bar back. Let your goals be known. No one can help you if they don't know you want help.

My first butler hotel job came through an agency but only after I had a couple of Houseman jobs. My first job in the service industry was fifty years ago, as a busser in the Golden Nugget Steak House, Downtown Las Vegas. The casino was owned by a man named Wynn. And, as I stated earlier, my last butler job was at the Bellagio, which was owned by a man named Wynn (father and son!)

You may want to move out of your area to be nearer a more affluent community such as Beverly Hills, Newport Beach, Palm Springs, Las Vegas, on the West Coast—New York or Miami on the East Coast. Your local library may have newspapers from the above areas. Check out the Sunday editions. Use the Internet.

Be prepared. Have a decent resume prepared. Dress appropriately; preferably a suit, white shirt (or blouse), dark tie and shined shoes. Get a haircut or set. Check for "coffee breath"—ugh! Cut your nails and lay off the fragrance! No cologne or perfume—during interviews and on the job. Oh yes, ladies, women butlers are very much in demand! Two of the best butlers who ever worked for me were women.

If you decide you want to pursue employment as a butler, houseman, etc., please know the day will come when it dawns on you: "Oh my God, I'm a servant!" That has to be "O.K." My day of dawning came on the very first day of my first job. I was forty-two years old. I decided I wasn't really cut out to be the business type and what I really wanted to do was stay home and play house. Unfortunately the pay scale on that job is "0"! So, I thought, I'll play house for someone else.

I saw a small ad for Houseman in the local paper and made the call. This was in San Francisco, circa 1976. I was interviewed by the real estate agent who had sold this large, five bedroom—six bath, four story home, to a family from Ohio. Oh my! But what the hey—I was offered the job and I took it. So there.

I met my new employer, his wife and five sons on the day we all moved in together. I was sitting on the steps when they pulled up in a caravan led by a huge moving van. We all spent the day unloading (manual labor—ugh).

Late evening found me on the floor putting away pots and pans in the kitchen, when in walked Mr. Cohen. In a casual tone he asked, "How about a scotch and soda?" Thinking, "How thoughtful" I replied, "No thanks. Maybe I'll have a beer later." (I really don't like scotch anyway.) To which Mr. Cohen replied, "No, Larry—for *me*." "Well, who did he think I was? . . . his *servant*?" Yes indeed, that's exactly what he thought. It takes awhile but you'll get the hang of it.

By the by, that's the reason most people do not make good waiters. They can't accept they are "serving", as in "service", as in "servant"!

I had a tiny little room and bath in the basement. I was the only staff except for the laundress who came on Wednesdays. Six days a week, I worked twelve to fourteen hours a day for the princely sum of four hundred dollars a month. When I left a year later, I was replaced by a staff of three. I did all the cooking and cleaning. (I learned to hate white carpets.)

The butlers in a private home are usually hired by the lady of the house (and fired by the Head of Security). If you are hired, they may help you with moving expenses. They may offer the use of one of their cars, they may want you to "live in" and then again, they may do none of the above.

Personal behavior when interviewing

1. No gum chewing
2. Leave the expensive jewelry at home
3. Don't mess or fuss with hair
4. Ladies—no cleavage. Modest, but elegant, in dress and not too trendy, please (and thank you).
5. Do not accept food or drink. A simple," No, thank you" will do.
6. It is a very good idea to have a pair of patent leather shoes.
7. You may be asked such questions (as I have) . . . "Can you draw a bath?"—Yes.

"Can you arrange flowers?" "Can you cook?" "Yes!" Please note, with regards to cooking, if you don't, can't or won't cook; say so. On the other questions . . . of course you can, but you may never have to. They just like to ask silly questions, to see what kind of an answer they will get!

Every situation is different, each job has yet another description. One thing is for sure—your interviewer, whoever it is, will lie to you. "We hardly ever entertain." That would be the truth if you think two or three times a week institutes "hardly". Just be prepared to work no matter what they throw at you. Your employer does not like to see you sitting around idle.

If you start as a live in, know that usually means you are "on call" at all hours. So, on your day off, get out of the house and get out early—before Madam asks you to run a few chores.

And, whether you live in or out, don't make plans too far in advance to attend that concert or see that show. Sure as hell, Madam is "having people in" that night. Just grin and bear it.

Stay out of the cookie jar, the refrigerator and any other hole or crevice where you don't belong. Without a specific invitation, you are not usually welcome to the boss's larder (i.e. groceries). Please be assured it will be noticed. You need only be called on it once to understand how embarrassing it can be. Been there, done that.

The Interview

The day before, wash your car and clean up the inside too. More than once I have had the prospective employee follow me out to my car after the interview to check it out.

The Night Before

Lay out your wardrobe, check for holes, wrinkles, etc. Check shoeshine. Inspect underwear and socks. No stains or holes, please.

There are two reasons to do the above. First, you won't be rushed and secondly (after you have showered) you will feel fresh and all together when you set out.

Upon arrival, don't block the driveway and don't walk on the lawn. Someone may be watching.

Once, on a first interview, I went way around the lawn to take the path into the main house. It was mentioned and appreciated. Someone was watching.

At the House

Never be the first to offer your hand for a handshake. Refuse any drink or food. Remain standing until offered a seat. Reply "Yes, Sir" or "No, Ma'am". I had a sign over my desk when training butlers stating, "No problem is a problem."

Watch your language. Don't rattle on. Be succinct and precise. Answer any questions honestly. Don't get caught in a lie; it could cost you a job. Maintain eye contact and, please, smile! Relax and enjoy the moment.

For the gentlemen: If you do sit and you cross your legs, make sure you show no flesh, i.e. wear long stockings.

Keep your nose just slightly up—but not too high. Cover your mouth when you (heaven forbid) yawn and your feet should be kept off of the furniture. You'll be just fine.

Good Luck and God Bless!

Learning the Language

Every business has a language. So too does the business of buttling.

Below is a list of what is unacceptable and absolutely must go, with no exceptions. Included is a listing of acceptable replacements. Take your pick or use all of these.

Note on language: it is never, ever, appropriate to speak in a foreign language in the presence of anyone who doesn't speak that language, when all who are present speak English.

Amateur vs. Professional—(It makes all the difference in the world)

Amateur:	Avoid these phrases at all costs
Professional:	Rehearse and use these guest-friendly phrases instead.
Amateur:	"No Problem!" (Absolutely the worst!)
Professional:	"Very good, Sir/Madam." "Certainly. I'll see to it immediately." Or "You're welcome." (What a concept)
Amateur:	"Yeah."
Professional:	"Yes, Sir/Mr./Mrs. Jones."
Amateur:	"Sure," or even worse, "Shurr."
Professional:	"Of course, Mr./Mrs. Blank," or "Very good, Sir/Ma'am."
Amateur:	"You bet!" "Okey-dokey" etc . . .
Professional:	"Very good, Mrs. Wilson," or "I'll see to it immediately."
Amateur:	"Oh NO!" "Not again!" or "Sorry!"
Professional:	"Thank you for calling that to my attention, Mr. Jones." (A good phrase to use when something is amiss.)
Amateur:	"Is everything okay?"
Professional:	"Is everything to your satisfaction?"
Amateur:	"How about [some desert, a cuppa coffee or something]?"
Professional:	"May I offer [desert, coffee, etc . . .]?"
Amateur:	"Are you through?" "Are you done?" "Are you still working on that?"
Professional:	"May I clear?" "May I remove?"

(Please do not reach at the same time. Wait for an answer!)

The phrase, "Take your time" is a definite no-no at any time.

Note: Never offer "or something." Always be specific.
Example: "For desert, we have apple pie, vanilla pudding."

And, of course, a professional would never use profanity of any kind. A guest's foul mouth is not an invitation for you to respond in kind.

You and the Staff

When you are new on the job and there is other staff, there are two very important things to ascertain:

1. Who's the Boss?
2. Who's the snitch?

Often, they are one in the same, but not always.

The Boss could be the Head Housekeeping or Madam's Personal Maid. It could be the more obvious Senior Butler or the Head of Security, if it is a large estate. You'll find out soon enough.

The snitch is a little harder to ascertain. If you never do anything wrong you might not find out for a while. But eventually you will. There is not much you can do about them except keep your nose clean and your mouth shut. Don't tell anybody anything unless you absolutely have to. No bragging, no secrets, no problems.

When you have made a mistake (and you will—we all do) say, "I made a mistake and used poor judgment. Please forgive me. It won't happen again." Memorize this phrase. It may be your salvation if you want to stay on the job!
P.S. And don't do it again.

You can say "No". Just say it in a nice way and have a very good reason for it.
I recall the daughter of the late comedian Phil Silvers, was getting married and her mother brought down her daughter's very elegant wedding dress and asked me to press it for her. I wanted to scream, "You've got to be kidding!" but I didn't. Instead I accepted the dress, kept it for half an hour and brought it back—untouched. She was delighted.

Answering the Phone and Front Door

Unless otherwise advised, it's "Rockefeller Residence." (And a good servant always carries a pen and note pad.)

Caller: "Mrs. Rockefeller, Please."
You: "May I say who'd calling?"
Caller: "A friend."
You: "I'm sorry, sir. Mrs. Rockefeller does not accept unannounced calls."
Caller: "Just tell her its Joe, the plumber."
You: "Very good, Sir. One moment, please."

Then check with Madam or Mr. to see if they are expecting the plumber. Then and only then, would you let someone unknown or unexpected to come into the house.

The above is just one script, but I hope you get the idea.

Only identify yourself if the caller asks who you are and it would be:

You: "My name is Larry. I am the Rockefeller Butler."

Never ever let someone into the house that you don't know or expect. It could be disastrous. On the call box:

You: "Yes, who is it?"
Visitor: "It's Jake, the plumber."

Don't forget your "Please and Thank You"s.
Use them early and use them often. Remember—it's "May I" not "Can I".

While at my first butler job at the Westwood Marquis, we had a young man check into the Butler Suites. I never knew why he was upgraded. It really didn't matter. Shortly after I had him settled in, here comes the family . . . (about twelve in all, as I recall). I could tell at a glance these folks were definitely not from Beverly Hills. We'll just leave it at that!

My guest invited them all to stay for brunch. As they were all agog and obviously smitten with his lavish suite, they weren't about to say "no"!

I took their orders; sandwiches, salads, hamburgers, cokes and such. I decided, "What the hell—let's pull out all the stops!" So I did. Flowers, silver, fine linens—the works.

After I had everyone served, I presented the guest with the check. He signed it and then reached into his pocket and pulled out a fist full of change and started sorting through for the larger coins (I assume). I reached over and put my hand over his and gently closed his fist around the coins. With a smile I said, "This one's on me. Enjoy!"

Tales from the Crib

I strongly suggest you never, ever pick up or touch a child of any age unless asked to do so, or in the case of an emergency. Play it safe. A butler is neither a baby-sitter, nursemaid nor nanny.

If children are to be involved, ascertain your place in this regard prior to signing on. If you are employed as a house person and you agree to child care and feel you are qualified to do so, then O.K. Otherwise, let your prospective employer know you are uncomfortable with this part of the job. It's only fair.

If small children are in the house, let them reach out to you in their own time. They will in due course. And with very small children and babies, don't get too close too quickly. Let them observe you from afar for awhile. It is never your job to discipline a child unless authorized to do so. Be careful in correcting a child but insist upon respect.

Encourage "thank you" and "please"—phrases fast becoming swear words in some homes. If you use "please" and "thank you" in a natural, normal way, the kids will catch on—a simple fact many of today's parents can't (or won't) grasp.

If you're a man, little girls need privacy, as do little boys, should you be a woman.

Note:

Make sure you have all the necessary phone numbers: doctors, dentist, pediatricians, parents work phone and cell phones, baby sitters, extra help, police and fire (usually 911), bartenders and any other persons you think you might need.

Things To Locate

First Aide Kit
Fire Extinguishers
Broom and Dust Pan
Cleaning Gear (Mops, etc.)

Stay Informed

Things to read—you can get them all at the library:

W Magazine
Town & Country
Architectural Digest
At least one daily newspaper
The Wall Street Journal
The New York Times (especially the Sunday Edition)

Around the House

Making a Bed: A Couple of Tips

Make sure sheets are high enough at the top. Otherwise the sleeper will have to pull the sheet up and out in order to cover their shoulders. Also, you don't want the blankets higher than the sheets; three or four inches below the sheet should do it.

You may also be asked to turn down a bed. It's not complicated. It's just this:
You remove all excessive and decorative pillows and then turn down the covers. One—sided for a single, both sides for a couple. Ask a maid at a local hotel to show you the details. I'm sure she will be happy to do so.

Watering Indoor Plants

A little splash of water won't do. If the plant needs watering, soak it good, making sure to drain excess. To test, poke a finger down into the soil an inch or so and if dry at that level—go ahead and water.

Cleaning a Mirror

Save the classifieds from the morning paper and use in lieu of a rag or paper towels. Don't overdose the window with Windex—a little dab will do you. Note: The paper needs to be "fresh"—before the ink is too dry. Try it, you'll like it!

The same is true if you are required (Heaven forbid) to do windows. In that case, you'll need the whole paper—Sunday Edition.

Packing a Bag

First, save those plastic cleaner covers in a safe place. Use one on each individual stem (especially in a garment bag). Be careful not to stuff or jam.

If a garment has straps, double or triple the straps on the hanger so that they are snug.

The Rolling Method: Roll jeans and sturdy clothing and pack first. Then roll and pack lighter, more delicate items, last. Wrap all the above in plastic bags. Place wrapped shoes farthest from handle and stuff the shoes with rolled socks. Rather than curl belts, place them around other items.

When packing a jacket, with the jacket facing you, place one hand on each shoulder and turn the left shoulder (not the sleeve) inside out. Slip the right shoulder into the left shoulder. The two front halves now mirror each other, the inner facing of the jacket is now outside and its sleeves are trapped inside the fold. Now lay flat, tucking top and bottom into other packed clothes. Or if bag is too small, fold in two and fill in with other items.

Zipper won't zip? Spray heavily with starch or rub with a candle

Marble Floors

The Second Butler in a large estate usually handles the marble floors.

Maintenance: Damp mop weekly with clean, clear water. Use a mild detergent if really dirty, wiping streaks with a damp sponge. As marble is porous, don't soak or let water stand too long.

Wine Stains

Treat A.S.A.P! Sprinkle salt or soak with club soda. On carpet, if stains remain, try a small amount of Hydrogen Peroxide. Pat on and then rinse with cold water. When spot is dry, vacuum up remains.

Quick fix on carpet: Foamy type shaving cream. Sponge on and then rinse with cold water and then vacuum when dry.

Flower Arrangements

First, check to see what supplies are available. Instead of that spongy green blob that florist's use, put a bunch of marbles in a net bag and set in container.

If your flowers are coming from the family garden, pick first thing in the morning. Cut flowers with a knife as scissors will crush stems. Wrap in a damp paper towel and once indoors, put into water you have drawn prior to picking (so the water will be at room temperature). Now cut stems with a sharp knife and remove any foliage that would be below water level.

When arranging long-stemmed flowers in a wide-mouth vase, you can use plastic hair rollers to stabilize. Keep your arrangements away from A/C and out of direct sunlight.

Footnote to arranging flowers: *See "Rising to the Occasion" by Edith Hoyard and Wallace Pinfold for a detailed account.

Cleaning the Chandeliers

Now here's something to keep you busy while the family is off on holiday in the South of France.

You'll want to protect the floor using old cloth toweling, newspapers and or paper towels (it gets a bit messy). Now, cover each socket and bulb with twist tied small plastic bags. Spray entire fixture and pendants with enough window cleaner to saturate, creating runoff. Let drip dry and then polish with a soft cloth. Fun stuff!

Tips on Cleaning and Polishing Silver

On delicate, intricate designs, Heloise suggests using a mascara brush and using a double-faced powder puff for regular polish.

Wash and dry silver pieces before polishing. The best was to polish tarnished silver is by hand rubbing it with commercial polish or a paste of baking soda and water. Use a string with polish and rub between tarnished forks. Rub the polish lengthwise (not in circles or crosswise) using a soft, dry cloth. Rinse first with soapy warm water and then clean warm water, making sure no polish remains. Dry with soft cloth or chamois. (Note: Linen and dishtowels will scratch/damage the silver.)

That Company Car!

Often your employer will offer and provide a company or house car for shopping errands and even for use on your day off. I've had two Mercedes (one four-door and one 500 SL convertible), a Lincoln town car and a Corvette, amongst others. I want to offer my experience and relate a horror story, in this regard. I got in trouble twice and avoided trouble several times.

First, with the Mercedes Sedan, I had the side window broken out one night when I was parked in a questionable neighborhood. Thank goodness Madam was out of town and I just happened to have a friend in the glass business. I had it redone at my own expense and Madam never suspected a thing.

A second event happened one night when I lost the keys (or rather they were stolen, but that's another story) to this same vehicle. I called a blacksmith, and I'm here to tell you, you cannot unlock a Mercedes without a key! So, I had to have the car towed home. Needless to say, Madam was not very happy about that little episode.

My third adventure involved taking the town car out of town. I suppose that town cars are meant to stay in town!

The problem and the point here is: Always get permission before using your boss's vehicle for any use out of the norm. That's what I failed to do. I drove the car out of town to visit a nearby city and then I compounded the error by blabbing about the trip to the rest of the staff. Needless to say, Miss Smith couldn't wait to run and tell Madam. I bought my own car the next week, as requested!

And now, for the horror story to put the foregoing to shame. I'm just so grateful it didn't happen to me.

A Horror Story

A Beverly Hills Houseman went shopping in Madam's Cadillac. On his way home, via Santa Monica Blvd., he made the near fatal decision to pick up a hitch hiker, out of the kindness of his heart, no doubt. As soon as the new "friend" got in the car, he produced a knife and demanded to be taken to the house. When they got to the house, he tied up the houseman and Madam, looted the house and drove off in the Caddy! They were so lucky to have come out of this one alive, don't you agree?

So let the message here be; remember it's not your car. Your employer has been kind enough to provide it for your use. Treat this kindness accordingly and, by all means, communicate and say "thank you" frequently!

Always act as though your boss is standing right behind you. This way you will not ever get caught because you won't be doing it, N'est Pas?

Never snoop or pry. Mind your own business and never share your personal "stuff' with your employer. You will be surprised at how disinterested they are that your cat died.

I worked for a man in San Francisco, a world famous designer (now deceased) whose previous houseman had been with him eighteen years. He never even knew his man was married until after the houseman had passed away. He didn't know and he didn't care. And so it goes. Remember, they forget your name the minute you are out of the door.

Car Care

A houseman may be expected to wash and wax the car. Ask about car care during your interview, if houseman or butler. You may need to keep record of maintenance etc., usually not a problem.

Personal Wardrobe

1 or 2 Black or Dark Blue Suits
3 or 4 plain collar white shirts
2 black, plain ties
2 pairs plain (and comfortable) black shoes (alternate every other day)

Personal Equipment

Small note pads and several pens on your person at all times while on duty.
A shoe kit with brown, black and white paste (no liquid polish please)
2 lint rollers (at least two)

Note:

After you use a lint roller, do not remove the used section (that has the lint on it). If you do, you'll expose the new, fresh section and it will dry out. Remove it next time you use it.

Uniforms Provided By Employer

Unless you are a very young Asian, mandarin collar jackets are inappropriate no matter what your title; be it Houseman, House Boy (ugh) or Butler.

Security

This is a biggy—very important if you live-in! Of course large estates usually have security but where you have a butler/houseman, cook/housekeeper situation, probably not. Therefore, you will want to be very aware of what the procedures are, who has the keys to what, alarm systems, codes, etc.

The Noise Factor

Most, if not all employers want and insist on a quiet household. A lot of giggling and laughter coming from the kitchen indicates somebody is not working (and that's what you are paid for!) So keep it down and always walk away from an argument or any encounter that would be too boisterous. I've seen more than one person fired over just such behavior.

Your Own Quarters!

Always be ready for inspection. Take the time to straighten and hang up before you go to bed. That's also the time you'll want to make sure your uniform and shoes are ready to go for the next day. Check your nails, etc. Even on your day off, your room should be spic and span.

Speaking of days off, you may be asked to do a chore, pick up laundry, drop off a book at the library, etc. It's all part of the joys of living in. Don't be upset, just do it and do it graciously.

Serving Meals

As a Butler, the proper way to announce dinner is "Madam is served." You only announce once, making sure Madam hears and acknowledges your announcement. This doesn't mean that everyone will drop everything and dash to the table. It is what it is and you can only do what you're supposed to do. The rest is up to your dinner guests and their hostess.

During dinner, the butler stands on the right hand side of the hostess, at the head of the table. You are also responsible for her chair when she sits down and when she gets up. If it is just family, you will probably not be required to be at her side.

These are the details you will have to ascertain. Since this will probably be an established household, most of these procedures are already in place.

Buttling OJT

After fifty years in the service industry (thirty of which were as a butler) I have come to one great conclusion and that is:

Every job is different, requiring different skills, different approaches and often a different attitude.

Flexibility and willingness to learn are the keys to success. I assure you these fine qualities will be appreciated. An aloof, know-it-all (phony accent etc.), will get you no where but out the door. Be yourself, be honest and open and know and obey the rules.

So let's move into the more practical aspects of this business.

Valet Service

You may be asked to press out something—slacks, a blouse, etc. Never take on something you can't handle i.e. wedding dress, velvet or pleated garments.

When pressing gentlemen's slacks, turn them inside out. Get a hand steamer. They work wonders on most every thing and you won't be scorching anything.

If there are stains, bring them to the attention of the owner. Pressing or steaming will cause the stain to set up.

Missing Buttons:

When sewing on a button, always go back and forth, north-to-south and south-to-south. Do not cross over (very ugly and unprofessional.)

Ironing

You might be asked to touch up a shirt for Mr. or a blouse or skirt for Mrs.

For a shirt:

Iron in the following sequence: shoulders, collar, sleeves and then back & sides. Use a spray bottle for those hard to flatten areas.

Ironing a tie:

Use a slightly damp towel, placing it over the tie and then apply the iron on the towel. Press and presto the wrinkles will be gone.

When clothes come back from the cleaners, get them off the cleaner's hangers as soon as possible and place them on wooden or plastic hangers. Remove all plastic and discard (discard carefully if there are young children in the house.)

Slacks should be hung by the cuffs.

A butler should never be asked to do laundry. A horseman—yes. Remember to sort by color and be very careful in using bleach. Raw bleach should always be diluted.

Remember softeners used in the dryer always leave a film. Wipe glasses with a towel and you'll see what I mean.

Check to make sure fragrances in soap and dryer softeners are O.K.—some people are allergic to them and may not want fragrances. It never hurts to ask and asking shows concern not ignorance!

You may be asked to keep a certain area (foyer, front steps, etc.) clean. This is acceptable and should be done carefully and thoroughly. A houseman is expected, in most areas, to clean, cook and serve. A butler does not clean and cook.

Again, before accepting a job, go over the duties with your prospective employer very carefully. Remember you are interviewing them too!

While you may not be a cook, one of the often-asked questions is, "Can you fix a light lunch?" Of course you can.

Another often asked question is, "Can you arrange flowers?" And one I've only heard once was, "Can you draw a bath?" Of course you can!

Professional Service

There are three major elements of the art of professional service. Everything falls into one of these three elements. They are:

Knowledge
Language
Attitude

By the application of improved knowledge and the use of correct language, an individual can improve their attitude and build confidence. Knowledge and language can be taught and attitude can be changed, if the student is willing.

Coming to work is just that—but it doesn't have to be a dreary experience. You can make it an experience of joy and excitement. Remember, you're a salesperson. Bill Gates is basically a salesperson. Donald Trump is a Salesperson.

Common Modern Service, Formal

Guests are seated, the guest at hostess' right hand is served first (unless it is the hostess who is also guest of honor. Then she is served first—but only then.) Serve down the line towards the host (at foot of the table). Go past host, to hostess' left hand side and serve down to the host, again. When only host and hostess are left, serve host—then hostess comes last! Got that?

Very Modern Service

Ladies First! Remove in the same order as above.

Serving Styles

There are several serving styles and I just pass them on as information: knowledge is power my friends. For a closer look, see Amy Vanderbuilt's <u>Complete Book of Etiquette</u> published by Doubleday.

French Service:

The table is set with the food when the guests sit down

Russian Service:

The food is plated from a sideboard and served by the staff. Serve always to the left with the right hand. Remove from the left, to the left.

Table Setting

Know all the various pieces of silver, china, glassware, etc. used in table settings. Browse the shelves at your local library for books on table manners and table settings. Visit fine china and silver shops and departments at upscale department stores. Ask for and study any brochures they may offer.

Silver Setup

Set forks at the guest's left, knives and spoons at the right.

A note to you knaves on knives:
All knife blades should be facing inward, toward the dinner plate, never outward (too threatening.) Dessert spoon and fork are placed on the table at the head of the plate, with spoon in the lower position, bowl end facing left; fork is placed above spoon, tines facing right. Got it?

The guest should work the set up from the outside inward, but don't count on that happening all the time. Just set up the needed silver and let them have at it.

If your guest sets the knife and fork tines down, parallel across the plate, with the handles near four o'clock, this if the formal way of signaling they are done. Even so, be sure to ask, "May I clear, Miss Dennis?"

Napkin Folding

Elaborate napkin folds are old-fashioned, unsanitary and fussy.
Management please take note:
Simple folds are easier, faster to do and are much more elegant than swans, et all. I have spoken.

Wine's World

Wines & Liquors:

There are all kinds and many colors, from aperitif to deserts. (Champagne is a desert wine!)

Aperitifs: (before a meal) would include Sparkling Shiraz and Sherries.

With a meal:

Reds and whites . . . so many to choose from! Let you host and hostess make these decisions.

After a meal: (including some liquors) Drambuie, Galliano, Apricot Brandy and other brandies, sparkling wines and Santermes.

When new in the house, ask for permission to inventory the "booze supply" so you'll know what's on hand. If you have some expertise in this area, don't be afraid to advertise it; such as "I make a great martini!"

Red wines should be opened at least twenty minutes before serving. That is letting it "breathe". And speaking of open; get yourself a first-rate cork screw, i.e. "nothing cheap." Cheap doesn't work. Believe me, I know.

For just a whole lot of details, see <u>What to Drink With What You Eat</u> by Andrew Dormenburg.

Out the Door

Getting fired is never fun, but sometimes it's not your fault and, then again, it is! It's always shocking to be let go ("Sorry, it's just working out" is the nice way—"You're fired!" is the not-so-nice way) especially if you feel you are doing a good job. Please know that there are those rich people who just love to hire and fire people.

Mrs. Jack Warner (the Fifth Warner Brother) and now Time—Warner, would ring me up every now and then and ask if I were busy; if not, could I come work for her as she was planning to entertain soon and needed extra staff. I learned never to unpack. I would move into the Staff Quarters (all the furniture was covered in plastic) and just leave my suit case open and operate that way for a couple of weeks or so. Of course, she never did entertain and I would be on my way again. Oh well, it was fun while it lasted.

Her estate was high on a hill, with Versailles-like gardens, Olympic size pool, tennis courts, seven hole golf course—none of which were ever used.

In the basement was a complete home theatre with full stage and kitchen. The stage was ringed with the many Oscars Warner Brothers had won over the years. Occasionally, I would sneak down and play with Oscars (again, a no-no) "I want to thank all the little people", of which I was one!

She had a life size portrait of herself in the drawing room done by Salvador Dali. Now that's rich and famous. She was truly one of the last Grand Dames of Old Hollywood. When she passed, the estate was sold to Geffen, the record man, for 43 million! He tore it all down.

Early on, while I was still a houseman, I was hired for a Ford hire (he wasn't a Ford, just had a whole lot of their money). He lived in this rather crappy mansion in Newport Beach but it was right on the water where he parked his 125-foot yacht. There was also a rather nice live in girlfriend and her six-year-old son.

I had only been there a couple of weeks when the girl friend had advised me that "the boss" had gone down and fired the entire crew and several contract people who were restoring the boat. No reason, he just liked firing someone. Said girl friend advised either she or I were probably next. It was me, first.

He walked up to me one day while in the middle of fixing a rather superior lunch and said "You're fired. You have twenty minutes to pack and get out." And so I did.

Three weeks later, Miss Girlfriend called me and said she was working at a message parlor.

Short Timer

There are times when you just don't have a good match and for any number of reasons the job just doesn't work out for you and/or your employer.

Case in Point:

Very early on I was very eager to take any job that came along that would allow me to advance toward my goal of being a real Butler. So, when my agency called me in Palm Springs, doing pretty much of nothing, I jumped at the chance to move to Beverly Hills for employment as a houseman for the Newly Wed Mr. and Mrs. Ron Samuels. (He was her agent, she's Linda Carter nee Wonder Woman.)

All went well for the first couple of weeks, until one morning I woke up early to the sound of someone banging around in the kitchen. So I pulled on a robe and went to investigate. There on a stepladder was the Mother-in-Law rearranging the cupboards. I knew then that I was not long for this job and neither was Ms. Carter. We both were out the door very shortly. Sad, too; I really liked her and she was great fun. When we would go shopping at Gelsen's, she would actually stop traffic, she was so stunning—one of the most beautiful women in the world!

I understand she has found happiness as the wife of Robert Altman, the high-powered Washington D.C. lawyer. I certainly hope so.

Shortly after the above, my agency sent me for an interview with Mr. and Mrs. Robert Six. (He's the founder of Continental Airlines—She's Audrey Meadows—"Alice" on The Honeymooners.) I moved into their comfy carriage house, they gave me a little car to use and I was set for life. Alas, it was not to be.

I soon learned I was there just for the Holidays (Thanksgiving through New Year's). I did my very best and learned a great deal during my brief stay. They were both very nice but a few days after New Year's, I was on my way down the hill for the last time.

The message here, I suppose, is that it isn't always your fault. As F. Scott Fitzgerald once wrote, "Let me tell you about the very rich. They are different from you and me." And so they are. Of course you will always know when you're fired for cause. Live and learn and move on.

When you are leaving on your own and, hopefully to new and better employment, never slack off. That's the time to shine. Let me share a couple of examples.

Example 1: The Lazy Butler

I was the Butler Supervisor at a very high-end resort in Hawaii, on the island of Lanai, for a number of years. When I first went there, they had a two man Butler Staff, one of which was a mess—yes! He was either late or a no-show most of the time and when he did show, he was disheveled and hung over. Oh my, oh no.

Fortunately, he found another job on another island and left. That job didn't last very long and soon I received a call from a HR worker asking me for my recommendation for this individual. Sad to say, I could only reply that I could not recommend him for re-hire. That's the best and legal way to handle this kind of situation.

And now for the good news—

Example 2

I had been working in the Houseman/Butler field for about five years. I had decided to go back to school (I was only 50!) and took a part time job as Host/Night Manager at a fun restaurant in Venice Beach, in the L.A. area. I was there for about six months when I ran out of money and school all at the same time. I had to find a real job and quick! In due course, there was an ad in my "Bible" for jobs, the L.A. Times, for a butler job in the Palm Springs area. I, wisely in this particular case, advised my boss of the situation, knowing he would understand. I went to Palm Springs and interviewed and while I was there they asked if it would be okay to call my present employer and I assured them it was. So while I was standing there she made the call. When she hung up, she turned to me for a very long minute and then she said, "You know what he just said? He said "Larry is the best employee I ever had and I don't know what I'm going to do without him." And that, my friends, is a real recommendation. I still choke up over this one. Needless to say, I got the job. Life is about the choices we make. And we have to live with our choices. Choose Wisely, Dear Reader.

Section II

OH—THOSE ROYALS!

The Prince and The Porn

Then Heir to the Throne, and now, His Serene Highness Prince Albert and his Father, Prince Rainier of Monaco, were our guests at the Bellagio and although they were not staying on the Butler Floor, we did look after them from time to time. Late one evening, Prince Albert called and asked for a couple of movies. We called around to all the video stores and they were all closed for the night. The only places open were the porn shops. I so informed his Highness. His reply—"That's okay. Send me up a couple." That Prince, what a guy!

But wait, there is more.
Earlier in my career, at the Westwood Marquis Gardens (now a "W") in Beverly Hills, I had attended to his sister, Princess Stephanie.

This was during her fling with Rob Lowe, who kept bouncing in and out—of the hotel, that is. The Princess needed special attention as she kept getting nosebleeds. (Must have been the altitude since she was staying on the fourteenth floor.) But I digress.

Meanwhile, back at the Bellagio . . .

One evening, management decided to take the whole entourage on an "insiders tour" of the Casino. As Prince Ranier was in failing health, I tagged along in case he got a little weary of all this foolishness (after all he did own Monte Carlo, the most fabulous casino in the world.) About half way through the tour, his Serene Highness declared "enough" and I stepped in to guide him back through the casino. So here I was with a personage who at one time was the most famous Bridegroom in the world, when he married film star Grace Kelly. Of all the thousands of people in the casino that evening, I recall only one person giving the Prince a second glance. Noblese oblige, indeed, n'est pas?

Did you know there are over five thousand Saudi Arabian Citizens who can claim the title of either Prince or Princess? Of course, they are not all of the Royal Family.

Case in point, I had two Princes on my Butler Floor at one time and they didn't even know each other and had never met. One was third in line to the throne and one was just another Prince. The former was a member of the Royal Family and traveled with a large entourage, the later traveled with one assistant.

Another time, we had an older lady and her entourage who we knew only to be a Saudi Princess. It turns out she was sister of the King thus a member of the Royal Family.

Hi Mr. King!

How Do You Do Mr. King? Titles, etc . . .

You may never need and of the following but its nice to know.
So, press on dear ones:

USA—The President (Present and Past): Mr. President
Cabinet Members (Present and Past): The Honorable
Senate Members: Senator
House Members: Representative

Royalty:

The Queen: Her Royal Majesty
Queen Mother and Dowager Empress: Her Majesty
The King: His Royal Majesty

Other Ruling Monarchs

Ruler of Monaco: His Serene Highness

Grand Duke and Grand Duchess*
The Duchess of Litchlenster

*Also Title of the Children of the Russian Czar (from the Roman Caesar)

Note: Not all of the wives of Kings are Queens and not all husbands of Queens are Kings. Example: Queen Elizabeth and Prince Phillip.

His Majesty, the King of Thailand and his wife, Her Royal Highness, Princess Sirkit

Children of Royals:

The Princess Royal—A special title given to the King or Queen's Daughter for outstanding Service to the Throne.

Infant (boy) and Infanta (girl) children of the Rulers of Spain not heir to the throne.

Dauphin (French 1349—1830) is the King's eldest son.

The Heir to the Spanish Throne is the Prince of the Asturias.

The Heir to the English Throne is the Prince of Wales.

Note: There are also Pretenders to the throne ergo—Dom Dwarte, Duke of Braganza, Pretender to the Portuguese Throne, Grand Duke Vendimis, Pretender to the Russian throne (first cousin to the late Czar. Lives in Canada) and finally Henry, Count of Paris, Pretender to the French throne, Pretenders are just that—Pretenders!

In descending order:

Duke and Duchess—His and Her Grace
Marquis and his Marchioness
Earl and His Countess (Lord and Lady)
Baron and his Baroness (Lord and Lady)
Baronet (male or female) (Sir and Lady)
Knight and Dame (Example: Sir John, Lady Jane)
Their Holiness and His Holiness: The Catholic Pope, the Greek Orthodox Pope and the Dali Lama.
Dukes and Duchesses who are members of the Royal Family and in line for the throne are also Princes of the Realm. Fun stuff, huh? There will be a quiz!

Royal Titles:

Heir to the Throne can be anyone—a brother, a cousin, etc., to the current ruler.

You will also see titles listed in this style:

HRM—His or Her Royal Majesty
HRH—His or Her Royal Highness (Member of the Royal Family)
HH—His or Her Highness

Note on Titles:

The newest English Royal is now HRH Catherine, Duchess of Cambridge, married to HRH Prince William, Duke of Cambridge, son of HRH Prince Charles and The Late HRH Diana, Princess of Wales. Prince Charles is the son of HRM Queen Elizabeth II and HRH Prince Phillip of Greece, Duke of Edinburg.

Princess Catherine is now a member of the Royal House of Windsor.

HRH Edward, Duke of Windsor, was married to an American, who was twice divorced, named Wallace Warfield Simpson. Although she had the title of Duchess of Windsor she was not allowed the HRH title, even though she married the former Kind Edward VII of England. The Duke of Windsor was HRM Queen Elizabeth II Uncle.

*Also, Prince of Wales and Heir Apparent to the Throne.

Additional Notes on Titles:

The Title of Prince/Princess does not always indicate a Royal. Example: As previously mentioned, Saudi Arabia has something over 5,000 Prince and Princesses and they may be called "His and Her Highness" but only members of the Family of the King are "Their Royal Highness".

Dowager

When the Duke dies and his son takes the title, then he (the son) and his wife take the title Duke and Duchess. Thus, the widow of the old Duke becomes the Dowager Duchess. This process is true with all lines.

Princess Royal

This title is awarded to the Daughter of the Monarch, for special services rendered to the Throne. Princess Anne, Daughter of Queen Elizabeth II is a Princess Royal.

Posthumous Title, i.e. "Catherine the Great", title awarded the past Monarch, i.e. "George the Good" was awarded to her father by QE II.

Non-Royal Family—Prince and Princess
His and Her Highness
Your Highness
Their Highness

Other Titles

His Serene Highness Prince Albert of Monaco
His Serene Highness, Prince of Lichtenstein

HRH Grand Duke of Luxemburg

Note: a pretender to unoccupied or non-existing Throne has no special Title.

Section III

THE POP QUIZ

Questions

1. During a particular symphony (say in four movements) when is it appropriate to applaud?
2. During a particular symphony with, say three movements, when is it appropriate to chat with your neighbors (be it husband, wife, friend or perfect stranger)?
3. The First Violin usually has another title. What is it?
4. Why would the butler "iron" the morning paper?
5. What is the largest diamond ever found?
6. Name this year's . . .
   World Series winner
   NFL Champion
   Rose Bowl winner
   World Champion Basketball Team

7. What is the most exclusive club in the world?
8. What's the longest playing musical on Broadway and what show did it replace?
9. If Tiger Woods is the richest athlete (tournament winnings, endorsements, fees, etc.) who is the richest female athlete?
10. It's the Earl of Sandwich, so what is his wife called?
11. Name one other person, other than the Catholic Pope, who is called "His Holiness"?
12. What makes an Opera "Grand"?
13. We shout "Bravo" for a male singer, "Brava" for a female.
    What do we shout for an ensemble?
14. Who is the richest woman in Beverly Hills?
15. Who is the wealthiest woman in America (and probably the world)?
16. If Bill Gates is the richest man in the world, who is the second richest?

Answers

1. At the end and never between movements. This also holds true during an opera except it is expected that we applaud an aria. For a ballet, applaud a ballet sequence of consequence. (Do you love that line?!)
2. After the entire symphony is over. P.S. It's very rude to fiddle with your program, open candy wrappers and "conduct" or generally bounce around!
3. Concert Master
4. To dry the i8.
5. Answer: The Cullinan (uncut) at 3,106.76 carats
   Cut from the above, Star of Africa at 530.2 cuts.
   It is in the Scepter of the British Crown Jewel (only used for state purposes.)
   In 1985, the above was super ceded by the Golden Jubilee, at 545.67 cuts, presented to Her Majesty Queen Elizabeth II of England.
6. Answer:
   I don't know—I'm retired!
   But if you want to be a working, professional butler, you should know. Hint: Here I'll mention again to read the local daily newspaper everyday including Sunday—cover to cover.
7. Probably the Yacht Club Costa Smeralda in Sardinia, founded by His Highness the Aga Khan. It's by invitation only with a $12,600 initiation fee, $2,520 annual dues and limited to 435 Members. Tres Swell!
8. "Phantom of the Opera". It replaced "Cats" (which replaced "A Chorus Line" . . . so there!)
9. Maria Sharapova, Russian Tennis Star, who lives in America.
10. Countess of Sandwich
11. The Dali Lama and the Greek Orthodox Pope.
12. It must have four acts and at least one ballet!
13. "Bravi"
14. Mrs. Marvin Davis—estimated at $8,000,000,000 Oil and Real Estate.
    The Men are $9,000,000,000 Kirk Kirkoran Casinos, Investments, real estate, movies and Viacom . . . and Sumner Redmar, estimated 7.5 Billion, Investments.
15. (No, it's not Oprah.) Christy Walton, widow of John Walton who was son of Sam Walton. Estimated at $15,600,000,000 her mother-in-law is next at $15,400,000,000.
16. Warren Buffet, Berkshire Hathaway Investments. (See note below) The last time I checked, his stock was right at $104,000 per share.

   *Note on Bill Gates (and second—place Warren Buffet)
   Occasionally the name "Carlos Slim" of Mexico pops up in the mix, but very hard to verify albeit he is a very, very wealthy individual.

Section IV

STORIES—WE HAVE STORIES!

The Ketchup Story

The Fabulous Mrs. Barbara Davis and her husband, Marvin, were entertaining a large dinner party at their palatial estate in Denver. The guests were from all over the world. At that time, Mrs. Davis owned 20th Century Fox Studios so there was a sprinkling of Hollywood types at the table.

As was the custom at the Davis table, steaks were served. Heavy, heavy steaks—oh my aching back. But I digress.

It was all very elegant and gala. At one point Mrs. Davis asked for some ketchup. It was always "please" and "thank you" at the Davis table. So, under much duress, I raced to the kitchen, grabbed a bottle of ketchup out of the frig, flew back into the dining room and blithely plunked it down on the table in front of her. It was only then that, to my horror, I realized what a faux pas I had made and it was too late to do anything about it.

After the meal was over, Mrs. Davis, as was her habit, came into the kitchen to thank the Chef and staff. I apologized profoundly and Mrs. Davis replied, "Oh Larry, I never even noticed."—Ya, right Mrs. D!

The Man in the Corner

In Hong Kong, the butler sits in the corner of your suite awaiting your every beck and call. I found this out when a couple returning from Hong Kong stayed with us in Hawaii.

When they checked in they immediately indicated they did not want any butler service. I found this very odd and upon pressing the situation, the couple was kind enough to relate the "Man in the Corner." After assuring them that the American butler doesn't work that way, they proceeded to work my tail off!

Remember, being a butler or any other service job is what you do—not who you are!

The American Slave

Hairdresser to her Highness

I met a delightful young lady at a Beverly Hills afternoon party some years ago. She said she worked for the twin sister of the ex-Shaw of Iran, in exile in the Los Angeles area. She explained that she would have to leave shortly to do her highness's hair for the evening. She told me she also had to o Her Highnesses hair every morning.

When I inquired about days off, she just laughed. She hadn't had a whole day off in nearly three years. Apparently she was very well paid for this inconvenient arrangement. We certainly hope so!

(That said—make certain to clarify your on duty hours, days off and vacation time at the outset. However, in this business nothing is set in stone. Be flexible and be prepared to change your schedule with little or no warning. It just comes with the territory. Many employers have a short memory. If you can't stand the heat, stay out of the kitchen.

Lovely Ladies and Kind Gentlemen

Time in the Tunnel

The Bellagio has a very private tunnel into the hotel reserved for the very rich and the very famous. Tres chic, no? Occasionally I was called upon to go to the tunnel to meet and greet arriving guests. I recall two outstanding occasions.

The first was a visit from Ms. Martha Stewart, here to do our Christmas trees and supervise the holiday décor. Our conversation consisted mainly of Ms. Stewart explaining to me her travel preferences. She has a time-share jet! (Why she chose to impart this information, we may never know. I doubt she will mention it when she writes her memoirs!)

The second, equally outstanding arrival was Ms. Elizabeth Taylor, the last real star! The poor dear was in a wheel chair, her feet so swollen she was barefoot. But shoes or not, here was a real live super star. Well, she absolutely glowed. Surrounded by a gaggle of young men, she had no chance to chat. Just being in her presence was quite enough.

I recall only one other celebrity who had that kind of presence and that was Mr. Frank Sinatra.

I'm often asked which personalities are nice and which are not. Who are the big tippers and who aren't! There are those who prefer, for whatever reason, not to offer a gratuity. Among those I recall are Chris Everett (tennis), Stefan Edgeberg (tennis), as well as Bryan Gumble and his wife Felicia Richard. I heard one of the floormen at the Bellagio remark "Somebody ought to teach that kid how to tip." He was referring to Tiger Woods who was sitting at a nearby Blackjack table in the Salon Privie.

Sometimes gratuities take an unusual turn.
Case in point:

When the owners of In & Out Burgers stayed with us in Hawaii, their pilot and stewardess brought in two cases of Dom, various sandwiches makings (bread, meats, cheeses, etc.) mustard and relish included! They stashed it all in their suite (The Presidential!) This quiet, reserved couple left two days later; All goodies were left behind.

Once, good behavior was my reward for my usual outstanding service. When we heard Ozzie Osbourne and family were due to arrive, I shuddered with fear and trepidation (oh, not really.) Turns out Mr. Osbourne was sober and on his best behavior. Actually the whole family was a delight—the kids were younger then, much younger.

Some guests, just by the sheer force of their personality, made my day. Among them were the late, great comedian Shecky Greene, Marvin Hamlish (the composer) and Robert De Niro.

And then there was the no-name tipper who stepped off the elevator one afternoon, mumbled something about, "Oh, so I'm supposed to tip now aren't I?" handed me twenty dollars and stepped back on the elevator and was gone. I never saw him again.

Far and away the best tipper of all time: the truly fabulous Australian media mogul, Terry Packer. (He left a 3 B Empire to his son James.)

He was the Highest of the High Rollers, Largest of the Whales in Vegas, known to have dropped "20 mill" in one evening. We loved him! He would tip a dealer $10,000, a cocktail waitress $5,000 and on and on. When he left, he would tip out the butlers (he brought two of his own butlers with him,)—$100,000 to be distributed evenly to all. He will be sorely missed, needless to say!

I've also been asked who were my favorite guests. I have two.

One is Carol Burnett and the other is Candace Bergen (although the latter was a guest in her mother's home) and both for the same reasons.

41

These are two caring and kind ladies, genuine and real. I felt more like a friend than a servant, but I never forgot my place and they made that place very pleasant indeed!

More Stories!

Thanks to my old friend Suzie of Palm Springs, I got my first taste of the celebrity world. Suzie had a small but classy catering business back in the late 70's. She was kind enough to invite me as an employee.

One of the first parties we did was for Jimmie Van Heusen, the great songwriter (two Academy Awards for "All the Way" and "High Hopes") and Frank Sinatra's great and good friend.

I must say Mr. Sinatra and his lovely wife Barbara, were always pleasant, although I must say Mr. S certainly liked his Crown Royal.

We also did several parties during the Symphony Season. (Yes, Dear Ones—Palm Springs does have culture!) And I recall Maestro Zubin Metah always thanking me when he was present at one of those festive post performance parties.

Meanwhile, back in Beverly Hills, a certain Sun Tan Lotion Company was noted for it's fun parties, particularly the gorgeous girls and celebrity participation. I lucked out and was asked to bartend one of these little gatherings in one of our larger suites at the Westwood Marquis. The place was packed. Tony Curtis, all in black, decided to keep me company at the bar as did Max Baer, Jr. (Jethro on the Beverly Hillbillies). There we were, the three of us, holding forth in a room full of some of the most beautiful young things in Hollywood. A very fun night!

The Best Deal in Town! (**Any** town!)

There is this fabulously wealthy Saudi Prince who bought this really fabulous mansion in Beverly Hills and hired a staff. He then bought the fabulous mansion next door and moved his whole staff into it. He stops off once or twice a year while on his way to fabulous Las Vegas, picks up most of his fabulous staff, flies them all in his fabulous Boeing 707 to fabulous Las Vegas with him and they all have a (all together now) fabulous time! Now that's a truly *fabulous* job.
P.S. In Vegas, he gives each employee a thousand dollars to gamble with.

The Bold and Sassy

Two gentlemen were hired on as Major Domo and Chef by a past employer of mine. This lovely family spent the winter in their Palm Springs "digs", which was also fully staffed. While they were gone, the two above mentioned fellows opened a catering business out of the family's kitchen and since the groceries, etc., were all charged to the family's account, profits were to say the least, outstanding. Oh yes, they got caught and are presently doing time. The give away came when they charged a five lb. tin of very, very expensive Russian caviar. That caught the bookkeeper's attention!

Stand Up, Sit Down, Shut Up

We had just finished a reception for Ginger Rogers.
I had worked all day pulling it together, it was late and I was pooped!

I had escaped to the kitchen for a quick sit down. I had no sooner sat down, when in walked the boss with a guest he was touring the house with.

I looked up and managed a holy smile and a "Hello—Nice to meet you" and off they went to finish the tour. As soon as they left, I realized that I had muffed the whole scene.

    #1—As I was not actually working at that moment, it was appropriate for me to
        stand up (sort of "at attention" if you will) which I didn't do.
    #2—I offered a greeting, which I should not have done.

The one thing I did do right, was not to offer my hand.

It is also inappropriate for the guest to offer their hand so don't feel put down if they don't, because they shouldn't—male or female.

I made a point to apologize to the boss first thing next morning.
I have no problem admitting when I am wrong. Actually it feels really good.
Try it, you'll like it!

The STAR WARS Crew

. . . At the Westwood Marquis B.H.!
No one knew if the original STAR WARS was going to be a success. Since the whole cast (except Mr. Ford) stayed with me for the whole week prior to the world premiere, I had a front row seat to their antics.

This was my first big celebrity splash and needless to say, I was all a twitter. Unfortunately, Princess Leia (Carrie Fisher) was sick in bed with the flu (or not) the whole week. Her mother, Ms. Debbie Reynolds, stopped in to cheer her up and I think she brought some chicken soup.

When Ms. Reynolds stepped off the elevator, I was immediately taken with how petite she was, knowing her unofficial Hollywood title, "The Iron Butterfly"! She had on a white turban—right out of the forties. All star, all class. When she announced, "I'm Ms. Reynolds, here to see my daughter' I knew there would be no small talk here, as I ushered her to Miss Fisher's Suite.

It turned out to be a fun week, worked my tail off and as we all know, the movie was a smash. And may I say, in my celebrity defense, so was I!

The Farmer and the FBI

To this day I have not come up with a good guess as to what these two agents might have been after. All I know is the two checked in, advised they were having dinner for three, and wanted a full bar installed in their Suite.

This was at the Westwood Marquis and Gardens, in Beverly Hills. It was my first job as a real Butler. The hotel is now a "W", but I digress.

It was a quiet night, so I was able to give the boys my full attention. I really put on a show for them; candles, silver, the whole smear. When their guest arrived I was most taken aback. Here was the grandfatherly figure, everything but wearing bib overalls and smelling of horse manure. How strange, no?

I can only assume they got what they were after because they couldn't thank me enough and one went to his own bank to come back with a very nice gratuity. Apparently the FBI knows everything except tipping.

The Two Ms. Bergens

For five years I enjoyed an insider's look at old Hollywood, combined with an occasional glance at the new Hollywood. Candace Bergen is the daughter of Mrs. Edgar (Francis) Bergen. Candace's father was a huge star in the 30's and 40's (along with his side-kick dummy—Charlie McCarthy).

While Mr. Bergen was a very handsome man, Candace gets her looks from Francis. Mrs. B was a Power's model (very big in the 40's and 50's) and fledgling singer. She gave it all up to be a wife and mother.

I worked as a Major Domo and Driver for Mrs. Bergen in her lovely little cottage in Beverly Hills. She was selling the big Bel Air house just when I was hired on.

Now, I must tell you Mrs. Bergen could be very difficult at times, but usually we got along fine.

Some of Mrs. Bergen's close friends were the Robert Stacks, Marie Windsor ("Queen of the B's"), Irene Dunne, The Justine Darts (Dart Industries), Mr. and Mrs. Ricardo Montabalan, Cliff Robertson, Mr. and Mrs. Tony Martin (she's Cyd Charise), The Jimmy Stewarts, etc. They would all gather at our house from time to time for drinks and then it was off to some gala event.

I would usually drive and drop them off. Mrs. B would call when they were ready to come home. I remember one event, I was standing out front waiting to gather up my tribe and take them home. As I looked around, Johnny Carson was standing right behind me, chatting with Gregory Peck. In front of me was Mohammed Ali, waiting for his Rolls Royce. It was all so Hollywood.

Candace lived in New York at that time, married to the late great French director Louis Malle (director of "Atlantic City" and "My Dinner With Andre"). I remember when their daughter Chloe was born. Chris was in school at San Diego State. (Most people don't know Candace has a younger brother, Chris, a terrific kid who is now a film editor in Hollywood.) Both Candace and Chris came home for short visits, always a delightful time. The rest of the time it was just Mrs. B and me! And Hollywood's Old Guard.

Let's see, Candace in NYC and Chris in San Diego—do we see a pattern here? Remember I said Mrs. B could be difficult?

A little known fact about Mr. Malle. He was very wealthy outside the movie industry as an Heir to a French Spice (salt) Fortune. Someone once asked him what kind of movies he would make if he (Louis) had 100 Million Francs. Mr. Malle replied, "But I already have 100 M Francs." So there!

Here Comes the Gates Family!

While employed as Butler Supervisor at the gorgeous Manele Bay Hotel on the Hawaiian Island of Lanai, we got word that Bill Gates and his Fiancé, Melinda, were coming to Lanai for their wedding. Vision of riches danced through my mind . . . who knows where all this may lead!

The whole affair was rather subdued, except for Warren Buffet, who was great fun. Of course, there was a ton of publicity—most of it fabricated. Mr. Gates did not buy out the whole hotel. He bought all rooms not occupied or reserved. He did not rent all the helicopters in Hawaii—just those on Maui (across the bay). The wedding itself, took place on the golf course, overlooking the sea.

As we arrived (Mr. Gates, his Best Man and I) via golf cart, a single large cloud shaped vaguely like a pillow, floated over the site. The sun was low in the West. Just as the ceremony started, the rays of the sun hit the Pillow Cloud, causing it to shimmer. What can I say?

Mr. Gates' mother was very ill, so the whole affair came off with the proper decorum. The gracious lady passed away shortly after.

Also in the wedding party was Katherine Graham, owner of the Washington Post, another lovely lady.

One of the honored guests never stayed in the hotel. That would be Paul Allan, Microsoft Co-Founder. He had his enormous yacht parked in the harbor, where he held forth in regal splendor. Show off!

When I drove the newlyweds to catch their waiting private jet (one of several parked there to whisk their guests to the four corners of the earth) it was apparent from their conversation that Mr. Gates had not only gained a wife, but had a new business partner.

When I would serve lunch to Mr. Gates, he would usually be reading a book. He would look up, nod and go back to reading. Just a bit aloof or possibly shy. I don't recall him appealing directly to me at any time during the stay except at the airport departure when we forgot his golf clubs and bag. Oh big to-do over that one, I'll tell you. But in the end, it was all forgiven and they were Aloha and off we go.

Oprah and Stedman Come to Hawaii

While holding forth on Lanai at the Manele Bay Hotel, we welcomed our most celebrated celebrity, Oprah Winfrey and companion, Stedman Graham to the Butler Suites. The rest of her entourage stayed elsewhere in the hotel.

Ms. O stayed in the Presidential Suite and the suite next door was reserved exclusively for her Stairmaster. It was all very relaxed and we felt no pressure from her or her staff. When they were preparing to depart, having been discovered by the paparazzi, Mr. Steadman called me in to handle the gratuities for me and my staff (I was Butler Supervisor). Before he could tip us out, Ms. Winfrey marched in exclaiming—"Oh Stedman, you don't know how to tip!"

She was very generous and we were all sad to see her leave early!

Wayne, The Fonz & Joe Montana—all in one day & at one time

I got very used to celebrities very early on in my career. I always gave the best service to all my guests and that always seemed to work well. But every now and then we would pack them in (especially Holidays) and we would be under additional pressure.

One of those days of pressure occurred in Hawaii during Christmas. We were packed and I was handling three different arrivals. They were Wayne Gretzky, with his lovely wife and family, Joe Montana and his wife and family and "Fonzie" himself, Henry Winkler. Fortunately, all three were frequent guests and they were so very kind. They all left their egos at the door, we all worked together and in no time (well, almost) we all settled in for Happy Holidays!

Speaking of Happy Days, Henry Winkler and I connected some years later. Mr. Winkler was a guest at the Bellagio and we reminisced about old times.

Arnold in Drag

Arnold and Maria Schwarzenegger (and family) were frequent visitors to the fabulous Manele Bay Hotel on Lanai. I spent seven happy years there as the Butler Supervisor.

Although the Schwarzenegger Family never stayed with me, I did often greet them and get them settled in.

The view from my office overlooked the pool and the beautiful bay.

One day I looked down on the pool and there was Arnold splashing about with his children. All was very normal looking except Arnold was wearing a very bad wig. It turns out, apparently, that he thought this would be a very clever disguise. Since he was also wearing a Speedo, it was pretty hard to disguise that incredible body. Oh well, Arnold seemed happy with it all!

At the Bellagio

We were preparing for a sit down dinner for Rupert Murdock (Australian and now U.S. Citizen—Media Mogul Fox News, etc.) and his son guests and wife in the formal dining room in his High Roller Suite. I noticed, someone had placed the coffee spoons on the saucers of the coffee cups. I loudly proclaimed, "What idiot put these spoons here? They belong just right of the knives."

Three days later I was moved to the very boring graveyard shift. Turns out, it was my Boss who was the culprit! Do you see a lesson here?

Hollywood's **Most Popular Star** and for Very Good Reasons

It's a very rare occasion when a celebrity arrives and no one knows about it. Especially if they are a Major Movie Star! (Whether incognito or alias.) In my thirty years, it only happened once and that was at the Bellagio in the first year.

Several times I made deliveries, brought in some lunch for the well-behaved children and chatted briefly with the Mrs. Who I did not recognize. Shame on me. None of us saw Mr. for that whole week. Then on Tuesday, they check out but not before they stopped at the Butler's Office to say "Thank you and Goodbye." And so we bid adieu to Tom Hanks, his beautiful wife, Rita Wilson and their delightful children. It was the first, last and only time any guest had shown the Butler's this courtesy. Classy.

The Bar-B-Q

At the Bellagio, one of our high rollers decided early one evening that he wanted to have Bar-B-Q for about twenty people on his patio, poolside, in about two hours. This would require a couple of chefs, bartenders, wait staff and butlers.

The menu would include hors d'oeuvres and canapés to be passed by the butler—steaks, lobster salads, vegetables and desserts (cakes, pies, etc.) There was to be a full bar and wines with dinner.

All the above was to be set up and ready to go in two hours.

Somehow, through a series of almost miracles, haps and mishaps, we put it together with ten minutes to spare. When it came to the whales, we never, ever said "No"!

I have enjoyed this sharing. I never realized how fortunate I was to be of some service to all the people mentioned herein (Let alone the hundreds of everyday rich folks not mentioned).

I have one last story.

The Davis Family

Just once, it all came together, not perfect, mind you, but darn close. The imperfections are always part of what makes it good.

I received a call from my agency, advising they had a very special opening in a private home in Denver, Colorado. I had never been to Denver (it gets cold there) and had never heard of Marvin Davis. The agency assured me this was a golden opportunity so I agreed to go interview. The Davis' send their private jet to take me from L.A. to Denver. I was met by Davis Security at the airport and driven to the lovely estate. (Not huge mind you)

I was shown to the living room where everything seemed oversized. Could this be because Mr. Davis was 6'6" and over three hundred pounds? Could be!

Mrs. Davis, La Petite, arrived and I immediately fell in love. What a lovely lady. She was wearing a diamond ring big enough to skate on. She didn't have to worry about losing that rock down the drain.

Naturally she hired me and they promptly moved me into a really neat apartment (no body lived in). My duties were light. Serving Mrs. Davis her lunch, a little shopping, run some errands; that sort of thing.

Mr. Davis would arrive home right at 8:00pm with Mrs. Davis ready to greet him at the door. He was never late. They would go directly in to dinner. I would serve, clear and I was out the door.

There was a staff of twenty including security. Naturally, there were tennis courts and a huge pool (none of which were used by the family).

The Davis' also had a fully staffed home in the Palm Springs area. They spent most of the winter there, which left us very little to do. When they returned, in the spring, it was in time for the Annual Carousel Ball. I had been warned by the staff what a major job this was going to be. Turns out, the whole thing was catered and the staff sat on their duff and watched the proceedings. (There was a special check for each of us the following payday—for our "troubles".) I kept Mrs. D supplied with water (neither drank) and Mr. D with food (that he did do with great gusto). It was *that* kind of a job.

As Mr. Davis owned Twentieth Century Fox at the time, the place was packed with celebs. I had a moment to chat with Beverly Sills, my favorite Opera star. She introduced me to Donald Sutherland, who sent me off to fetch a drink for him. And a good time was had by all. And Mrs. Davis' charity, Juvenile Diabetes, made a killing.
So many memories, but my favorite was Christmas.

The Davis' gave me the nicest, most lavish Christmas I ever had. So many gifts, all very thoughtful and appropriate. When they decided to sell the house and move to B.H., (They had purchased Kenny Roger's estate for a reported twenty million, which was sold after Mr. D passed away for a reported forty million) it was time to move on. What a ton of great memories with a great family and may I say, "Thank you!"

A Day in the Life

I started my day at the Davis Mansion at 10:00am. By the time I arrived, Mr. D had left for the office and Mrs. D had had her breakfast and was usually on the phone. Or, perhaps, she was still in the security room checking out the day's arrivals. Everyday she would receive boxes from world famous designers, jewelers, etc.

Security would open the boxes and have everything laid out for her inspection. Mrs. D would pick out whatever she liked. Security would then box up the remainder and send them back. Belle, Mrs. D's personal maid of twenty five years, would pick up that day's selections, press them out, if needed, and take them to the "Wardrobe Room" and hang them up with the hundreds of other outfits, some with the tags still dangling from a sleeve or hem.

Please note: While I refer to her as Mrs. D here, I would never, ever, refer to them as anything but Mr. and Mrs. Davis in person or to others. Although the Head of Security would page "Mrs. D", I certainly didn't. This same Head of Security turned out to be the "inside man" to the famous Davis Jewelry Heist (to the tune of fifty million dollars worth) . . . but that's another story, for another time.

Mrs. Davis would call me in, after I had my breakfast, and give me a list to go shopping with. They had accounts everywhere! She always had "fresh cheese" on the list, everyday. Is there such a thing?

When I returned from shopping (I used one of the many cars—usually a Lincoln Towne Car—which I gassed up at our private, onsite, gas station) it was time for lunch.

Mrs. D usually lunched alone, although, occasionally daughter Nancy would join her. Nancy lived near by. Mrs. D always, and I mean always, had the same thing—half a roasted chicken, a dab of peas and a baked potato. After I cleared lunch, I was pretty much on my own to putz about until dinnertime.

They seldom used the "Big Dining Room" and chose the "Breakfast Room". Mr. D would arrive at 6:00pm and Mrs. D would be coiffed and looking lovely for his return after a hard day at the office. Mr. D drove the Rolls followed by security in another car. They would go in immediately to dinner.

I would serve dinner on a "high platter". Meats (chicken, beef and a chop or two) veggies (usually peas) and they would make a selection. I would retire to the kitchen and in about fifteen or twenty minutes, pass the tray again. After waiting another ten or fifteen minutes, I would pass the dessert tray, laden with an assortment of fresh baked goodies.

When they had finished dinner, they retired to their private quarters. I would set out a bowl of very special cheese and some rather ordinary Ritz crackers, bedside, for Mr. D to snack on as they watched T.V.

I would take the dinner from what was left on the plates, share the desserts with the rest of the staff that was still on duty and was out the door. We had one of the maids, who helped the chef, clean up.

By the by, with security, butlers, maids and yard people, we had a total of approximately twenty in and out throughout the day and night. Now I ask you, how good can it get?

Occasionally, we would entertain—usually a movie. There was a fully equipped theatre in the basement, along with a game arcade and a soda fountain. Mrs. D would have me call in a bartender, although nobody drank, have two maids standing by and there would be myself and another butler. Chef would prepare a lavish buffet, which just sat there as everyone seemed to be on a diet.

After they all filed out and went to their respective homes, Mrs. D would always say "Alright, everyone help yourself to whatever you like—take home the cakes and pie, please!" Always so kind, so gracious. Always with a "Thank you!"

Section V

DROP THOSE NAMES

And now 'tis time to play: "Drop That Name"

Often a guest will check in and be gone the next day. Occasionally I was to greet and room a guest (high end, high profile types) who were not staying on the Butler Floor, be it Penthouse, or High roller. Or, perhaps, they were just staying in another part of the hotel and I would be called upon to do special errands, such as touring or serving a special meal, etc. So here we go with Larry's (That's <u>Me</u>) List, by Hotel: A Plethora of People—love that word *plethora*, don't you?

The Westwood Marquis and Gardens (now a "W") in Beverly Hills, CA

Erté, the famous French artist—
He tipped me with a signed poster. At ninety-five years old, was still working out. How great is that!

Pete Rozell—Football Commissioner and his wife—
A lovely couple—All warm and fuzzy.

Ralph De Lauren—Car Guy
Rather Aloof and reserved.

Eric Heiden—Skater—Five Olympic Gold Medals and a real cute girlfriend

Alex Haley—"Roots"—a real gentleman.

Mr. Blackwell: I can't criticize him, now can I?

Akira Kurosawa—The Great (and very large) Japanese Director

Bob Denver: Came off the elevator with a handshake and said, "Hi, I'm Bob Denver and this is my brother Bill. Can you get us some beers?"

Sally Struthers (All in the Family):
She and I threw a surprise party for her husband. She was pleased! All too Gala—just the three of us!

Mitzi Gaynor: Movie Star and Entertainer—My "Golden Girl"

Anna Moffo: The most beautiful Opera singer that ever was!

Linda Grey (Actress)—A gracious Lady.

Occasionally, when it was slow, I was asked to help out with afternoon tea in the lobby. Bea Arthur ("Maude"—"Golden Girls") and the Presley Ladies (Pricilla and daughter, Lisa Marie) were guests I recall serving. All too proper, don't you know!

The Artist and Designer, Mickael Thoune, So Far So Good?

Brian Wilson—The Beach Boys
Easy to please and very laid back.

E.G. Marshall—A Martini always on hand!

Whitney Houston, her gal-pal, Mom and Dad (Mom is the great Jazz singer, Cissy Houston)

Hyatt Grand Champions Hotel, Indian Wells, CA (Palm Springs Area)

Linda Evans and pal, Yanni (Wasn't love Grand!)

Danielle Steele (Spent most of her time writing)

Henry and Ginny Mancini—He made beautiful music
On New Year's and got locked out of his Suite. Luckily I happened by and got them safely tucked away.

V.P. Dan Quale, family and all his F.B.I. guys. What a pain!

Lee Iacocca—Head of Chrysler—Very Big Wheel!

Tennis Players Rod Lever, Jimmie Connors and Martina Navratilova—always a fun group, but always business. No parties here!

Johnny Cash and wife, June Cash Carter—so well behaved in those days.

The Manele Bay Hotel, Lanai, HI

Rosie O'Donnell and crew shooting a movie. Ho Hum!

Robin Leach of "Life Styles of the Rich and Famous" shooting a segment starring Moi and Charles Shaughnessy (Mr. Maxwell on "The Nanny") Love that Show Biz!

George Foreman, guest appearance at small convention.

Paige Rense—Editor In Chief, Architectural Digest—Getting some well deserved "R & R" and recovering from the flu.

Larry Miller, Comedian, the early days. He's everywhere these days—Stage, Movies, T.V. et all!

Pianist Andre Watts—Gave us a lovely evening of beautiful music. I drove him to his concert site, we chatted a bit.

David Bowie and wife, the gorgeous Iman. She was certainly running that show!

Gene Hackman and Mrs. Hackman. I took them on a daylong tour of the Island. A fine couple they!

Roddy McDowell: Toured him and his friend. This is work?

Jean-Claude Van Damme: A real Family Man!

Peter and Arianna Huffington. Didn't he run for President? Oil Millions will do that.

Lee Atwater, Nixon's Press Secretary, then heading up a Drug Store Owner's Convention.

Reba MacIntyre and Family. So loving, so down to earth.

A slew of golfer's headed up by Jack Nicholas. Too many to mention and all business.

James Woods and Michael Douglas on a golf outing. Just a couple of regular guys!

Nicholas Cage and lady friend

Ed Asner (The Mary Tyler Moore Show) Hello and Goodbye and No Thanks!

The Billionaire De Voss Family (They are the Amway People)—ordered breakfast for all in the Presidential Suite. I was privileged to serve it. After I set it all up the extended family gathered around the table and held hands. I suddenly found myself a part of this saying of Grace. It just happened. Nobody asked, they just did it. So many great memories.

The Disney Clan, headed by Roy E. Disney, Walt's nephew and a dead ringer for Walt. They reminisced about the old old days parking their yacht in Manele Bay and swimming on Hulapoe Beach when there was nothing but pineapple on the Island.

David and Maria Murdock (The Dole Foods Folks). She's Jose Ferrer and Rosemary Clooney's daughter and George Clooney's cousin. They always stayed in the Presidential Suite, naturally, since they owned the place.

Dennis Quaid and his beautiful and talented wife, Meg Ryan, and son, handsome young Jack Henry, arrive by private plane—was that a pipes cub? I think so, but maybe not, oh well. Just folks!

John Elway and a bevy of lovelies. (He's late of the Denver Broncos.) All very private and hush, hush. One wonders, doesn't one?

John Tesh and new wife Connie Selleca on a secluded honeymoon—it's the only way, really.

The one and only Pat Morita, late of the Karate Kid Flicks. Fun Guy!

Ed O'Neil (Al Bundy on "Married With Children). I didn't know who he was!

John and Bill Tisch and the Tisch Family (They own Loews Hotels. All very polished and grand.

Diane Lane (actress)—"Who was that lady?"

The Bellagio Hotel, Las Vegas, NV

Ms. Bo Derek at a party. She thought I was cute!

Michael Jordan here for some R & R with the family.

Bruce Willis parading around the Salon Privé with his entourage of beauties. He would always stop by just to say "Hi".

Michael Jackson—he moonwalked down the hall for me!

Don Johnson (Miami Vice) at the Buffet

Paging Mr. Harrelson!

Kevin Costner, a frequent visitor at the Bellagio in Las Vegas, called me and advised he had a friend in the V.I.P. reception area and asked if I would pick him up and bring him to his Suite. Mr. Costner called me "Yoda" for some strange reason. He said Woody was waiting for me.

He had a dark, wool cap pulled down to his eyes and how shall I say it? Very, very, casually attired, especially since he was here to visit the always immaculate and impeccably turned out, Mr. Costner.

Arriving at said V.I.P. Reception Area, I immediately spotted Mr. Harrelson scrunched down in a far couch. I assume he was trying to avoid being recognized.

Since I am the clever one, I blithely strolled over to the couch, stood by the crouching star and in a loud voice paged Mr. Harrelson ala the old Phillip Morris Commercial! "Paging Mr. Harrelson—Paging Mr. Harrelson". He immediately jumped up and off to the elevator we flew. When Mr. Antonio Banderas joined Mr. Costner and Mr. Harrelson a little later, we had quite a party on our hands that night!

Tom Campbell—One of the great photographers of our times. I did some modeling for him (fully clothed, of course).

If you're not listed here, it's not that you're forgettable—you're not.

Epilogue

There are always exceptions to the rules; let common sense prevail.

Easy does it and flow from your heart. Let it go if you're hurt, angry or upset. Go lovingly through your shift and you will shine like the star you are. Have fun, be kind and enjoy what you do, as you do it. Give it your best and you'll be just fine.

"If you feel you cannot love everyone on God's Good Earth, then you must ask yourself these two questions, "Whom do you exclude and why?"

"Get Thee to a Library"

Bibliography

Beverage and Food Services. Culinary Institute of America.

Gold, C. & Wolfman, P. (2000). *The Perfect Setting.* New York: Harry N. Abrams.

Post, E.L. & Wink, L. (2000). *The Wine Guide.* Time-Life Books.

Wine Service. Culinary Institute of America.

Zraly, K. (2006). *Windows on the World Complete Wine Course.* Sterling.

Good Reading List for House Persons and Butlers

1. Anything by Heloise
2. Rising to the Occasion. Edith Hazard and Wallace Pinfold—Algonquin Books (Chapel Hill)
3. Haley's Hints. Rosemary and Graham Haley 3H Productions, Inc. Web: wwwhaleyshints.com
4. Reader's Digest Household Hints and Handy Tips by Reader's Digest
5. Better Homes and Gardens Household Hints and Tips by Better Homes and Gardens
6. The Little Know-How Book by Bob Scher, Harmony Books

Online

Have a question or two on wine?

Email F. Paul Pacult at <u>PACULT@INTERPORT.NET</u>

Or write Mr. Pacult at

GOOD LIBATIONS
1301 Carolina Street
Greensboro, North Carolina 27401

He's the expert and he invites your questions

Special Supplement

Dear Friends: I trust you enjoyed the forgoing offering.
I know I certainly enjoyed writing it for you.

I am now including a special supplement:
Selections from one of my other books, "Waiter International" which is available on
Amazon.com or from the publisher: Xlibris.com.

Since, in many cases, butlers, be they private or in hotel, often find themselves in a
waiter position, I felt the reader might find this supplement helpful.

So, enjoy and thank you for your support.

Larry O. Knight, Master Butler

Preface

Being a professional waiter requires a great deal more than just knowing how to present food. It requires knowing the language and having the attitude, backed up by both knowledge and skill.

It is our hope that this booklet will be of service to you as you grow and prosper in our chosen profession. Be proud of what you do, and always remember:

Being a waiter is what you **DO**.
Not who you **ARE. For the Server: Getting Started
Go See What it Looks Like**
Pick the best restaurant you can afford, and go more than once, if possible. Notice any differences in the service from one visit to the other. Ask questions; take notes.

Is this what you really want to do? Could you do a better job than most of the waiters you've had experience with?

Be critical of all you observe. Ask yourself what you would change and why.

If you're just starting out, ask for help. False pride will get you nowhere. Most people will be happy to give you hints and help if you drop the know-it-all attitude. In fact, I've found that most people, if properly approached, are very flattered by a request for help.

Very few people start out at the top, so be patient. And be on the alert for every opportunity to sharpen your skills. No matter how modest the operation, never work for a place you cannot be proud of, both out front and back of the house.

Knowledge is Power!

You will feel much more comfortable if your manner and knowledge are equal to, if not surpassing, that of those you serve.

Be aware that you can learn a great deal from your guests. It's okay not to know everything, and it's okay to ask the guest to explain to you exactly what he or she wants, if you don't quite understand.

Research

Know all the various pieces of silver, china, glassware, etc. used in table settings. Browse the shelves at your local library for books on table manners and table settings. Visit fine china and silver shops and departments at upscale department stores. Ask for and study any brochures they may offer

What Every Service Should Know

Silver Setup

Forks at the guest's left; knives and spoons at the right. A note to your knaves on knives: All knife blades should be facing inward, toward the dinner plate, never outward (too threatening). Dessert spoon and fork are placed on the table at the head of the plate, with spoon in the lower position, bowl end facing left; fork is placed above spoon, tines facing right. Got it?

The guest should work the setup from the outside inward but don't count on that happening all the time. Just set up the needed silver and let them have at it.

If your guest sets the knife and fork, tines down, parallel across the plate, with the handles near four o'clock, this is the formal way of signaling they are done. Even so, be sure to ask, "May I clear, Miss Dennis?"

Napkin Folding

Elaborate napkin folds are old-fashioned, unsanitary, and fussy. Management, please take note: Simple folds are easier and faster to do, and are much more elegant than swans, et al. I have spoken.

Tools of the Trade

Carry with you:

1. A very good wine bottle opener
2. A working cigarette lighter and two packs of matches (keep them in a "dry" pocket)

3. Two working pens and a note pad (again, keep in a dry pocket)
4. A crumbler (that little scoop for cleaning off tables after you have cleared, or as needed)
5. A cigar tip cutter (if appropriate to your particular situation)

You and Your Guests

Please keep in mind that your guests are your clients and patrons. Without them, you don't have a job. The guest may be wrong, but it is not your job or obligation to point that out. Conversely, you are not always right. When a mistake is made, it is your job and obligation to promptly correct it to the complete satisfaction of all concerned.

Being a waiter means never having to say, "I'm sorry!" No matter what terrible thing you have done or mistake you have made. A professional waiter always says, "Please forgive me!" and keeps saying it until the guests actually do. (And they will!)

It's all in the Details

Describe everything you put in front of your guests, in detail, to the best of your ability. "The cream of Jerusalem artichoke soup, sir"; "Your crown roast of lamb with scalloped eggplant"; "Our garden-fresh braised baby spinach." Your guests may not listen to you, but you will have done your part.

And know your ingredients! Be ready, willing, and able to describe in detail the ingredients of every dish on the menu.* Your guests *will* ask, so be prepared. Many people suffer from serious allergies, and there are also religious and cultural concerns over certain ingredients. Do you homework.

If something is amiss—the restaurant is short-handed, the air-conditioning has gone awry, etc.-your guests deserve and explanation up front, not after the fact.

Give them a reason, not an excuse. Offer a freebie, if allowed, up front, and let them know you're on their side and will do all you can to keep things moving along. Remenber, "Please forgive us, but . . ." and do it *before* they get angry and hostile!

A Language Lesson

A note to owners, managers, and staff:

- Your first greeting should ALWAYS be "Welcome!"
- Your most important tools are your eyes! Look-see-act.

Amateur vs. Professional
(It Makes All the Difference in the World)

Amateur:	*Avoid these phrases at all costs.*
Professional:	*Rehearse and use these guest-friendly phrases instead.*
Amateur:	*"No problem!" (Absolutely the worst!)*
Professional:	*"Very good, sir/madam." "Certainly. I'll see to it immediately." Or "You're welcome." (What a concept.)*
Amateur:	*"Yeah."*
Professional:	*"Yes, sir/ Mr./ Mrs. Jones."*
Amateur:	*"Sure," or even worse, "Shurr."*
Professional:	*"Of course, Mr./ Mrs. Blank," or "Very good, sir/ma'am."*
Amateur:	*"Bye now" or "buh-bye"; And "Have a nice day," is about as tired as it gets.*
Professional:	*"Good evening/ good day, Dr. Brown."*
Amateur:	*"you bet!" "Okey-dokey." Etc..*
Professional:	*"Very good, Mrs. Wilson," or "I'll see to it immediately."*
Amateur:	*"Oh NO!" "Not again!" or "Sorry!"*
Professional:	*"Thank you for calling that to my attention, Mr. Jones." (A good phrase to use when something is amiss.)*
Amateur:	*"Is everything okay?"*
Professional:	*"Is everything to your satisfaction?"*
Amateur:	*"How about [some dessert, a cuppa coffee, or something]?"*
Professional:	*"May I offer [dessert, coffee, etc..]?"*
Amateur:	*"Are you through?" "Are you done?" "Are you still working on that?"*
Professional:	*"May I clear?" "May I Remove?"*

Please do not reach at the same time. Wait for answer!

And "Take your time" is a definite no-no at any time.

Note: Never offer "or something." Always be specific.
Example: For dessert, we have apple pie, vanilla pudding.

And, of course, a professional would never use profanity of any kind. A guest's foul mouth is not an invitation for you to respond in kind.

Where There's Smoke

If you have a smoker at your table, watch that ashtray. Never let more than two butts accumulate before you remove the ashtray and replace it with a fresh one.

House Policy

What is House Policy? You need to know what you can comp (offer without charge) to make amends for a mistake or an error.

By getting very clear on such company policy, you will appear to be the competent waiter you are.

Always maintain a clear understanding with management as to what you can or cannot do to rectify any unfortunate situation. In the following situations, what is house policy?

Example 1: The guest has eaten all of his entrèe and *then* complains it was awful.
Example2: The guest eats a couple of bites of entrèe and complains right away.

Credit Cards

Know which credit cards your company accepts and which ones they do not. Check all cards for the expiration date. If expired, call this to the guest's attention in a discreet manner.

If card company denies payment: again, discreetly advise the guest and ask for another card for submission.

Know, before the fact, if the company accepts checks, and if so, what kind: i.e., personal, corporate, third party.

---

*Host/hostess/Maitre D must know the menu as well as the servers do, and be aware of daily specials. They should also know the neighborhood, local points of interest, banks, shopping, and transportation.

And We're Off to "Never-Never Land"

Do Not Try This At Work

- NEVER cheat your employer, or your guests, out of what is rightfully theirs: your time and full attention to their needs.

- NEVER touch or lean against a chair, occupied or not, at a table, once the guests are seated. I have seen this rule violated in the very smartest restaurants. Is everyone so tired that they can't stand up straight? The only exception to this rule: Waiter may (and should) help adjust chairs for guests, upon their arrival and their departure ("May I?" or "Allow me").
- Please do not stand with your arm folded behind you, fist in the small of your back. That is okay in Europe, but is a sure sign of an amateur here in the USA. Keep your hands in front of you, or at your sides, after all, you may need to use them quite suddenly.
- Always check your tables as you pass by. Smile at your guests, and glance at the table to see if they may be in need of something, *before* they ask. Care.
- Please do not avoid eye contact when a guest is trying to get your attention, even if you're very busy. Acknowledge each guest and signal that you'll be with them in a moment, or as soon as possible. They will love and appreciate you for that small gesture of kindness.
- It goes without saying your guests should NEVER have to ask for more water, bread, or butter. But, of course, you knew that.
- NEVER touch a guest unless it is an emergency. For example: they are falling over or have stumbled.
- NEVER offer a handshake. If a guest offers his hand, be gracious enough to shake it.
- Avoid chatting with your guests, and NEVER, ever, interject yourself into any conversation going on at the table, as tempting as it sometimes may be. Do not laugh at or acknowledge, in any way, a joke of any kind that may be going on at the table, unless it is very obvious that you are included in the festivities. Save yourself from a very embarrassing situation by following the above rule.
- NEVER offer any personal comments about yourself, your family, or friends. Usually, the guest could care less about your personal affairs. Should a guest ask a personal question, answer as succinctly as possible and move on.
- NEVER say anything, anywhere, to anyone, which is derogatory about any guest, period! Your negativity can and will cost you money. A lot. Get over it, and get on with it.
- NEVER get too chummy with the guests. Familiarity breeds contempt.
  Ex: *Situation*: A guests asks you to call him by his first name.
  Solution: Say, "Please forgive me, Mr. Smith, it is against house rules." (Even if it is not, it should be against your own *personal rule*). Therefore, NEVER call your guests by their first names, even if they insist. As someone once said, "New friends don't tip friends," and it's true. Of course, *real* friends usually take very good care of us!

- NEVER discuss anything personal with other staff while on or near the floor or anywhere your guests could possibly overhear it. NEVER!
  Ex: Situation: Another staff member wants to chat while you're on duty, on the floor.
  Solution: "Let's talk about it on break, okay?"

Odds and Ends to Avoid

Don't fuss with your hair or uniform. Do not scratch an itch while on the floor. It is very unattractive.

Avoid really ugly shoes. Believe me, people notice these things. Wear plain, comfortable, black, dress shoes (no sneakers, please).

Leave your expensive rings and watches at home. Nobody tips Mr. or Ms. "Rich Bitch."

The Paragraph I Would Rather Not Have Had to Write

Do I really have to say anything about bad breath, dirty nails, unpolished shoes, wrinkled, frayed, or soiled uniforms, or chewing gum while on duty? If I do, you're in the wrong business. And please, Snow White and the Seven Dwarfs notwithstanding, no whistling. Thank you.

Don't Rush

Try not to appear frazzled, harried, or rushed, even on the busiest night of the year. The secret here is to *do one thing at a time and do it right.*

Be economical with your movements. Remember the old "take something out and bring something back" rule. If you do not mentally get ahead of yourself, staying instead in the *now*, you'll be all right. If you keep thinking ahead to all you have to do, chaos will reign supreme.

A Guest's Thanks

It is not appropriate, nor should it be expected, that the guests thank you every time you fill the water glass, or as you serve dessert, etc. A guest's "thank you" at the end of the meal, when paying the check, is sufficient if the quality of your service warrants it. And don't forget to thank *them* for coming: "It's been a pleasure to serve you. We look forward to seeing you again soon."

Into Action—and Away We Go

Checking In

Before you start the workweek, take a few minutes to copy down your schedule from the bulletin board. This eliminates the possibility of coming in late, which could result in disciplinary action. Be sure to check the starting time for your station. Also check the board for any new information that may have been posted.

You should be dressed and ready to work when your shift begins. Hands must be clean. You must have a pen, crumber, and wine opener before you start your shift. Your uniform must be neat, clean, and pressed. (See *Appearance*)

Opening duties include:

- Making sure the menu covers and pages are clean and neat.
- Making sure the menus contain the correct pages for lunch and dinner.
- Reviewing your reservations for the day and notifying servers of large parties.

Food Servers:

Before you go out to your station, check the kitchen for pertinent notices and specials. If there is no description of how the specials are prepared, ask the chef or manager.

The server is responsible for every aspect of service including the initial approach to the table, greeting the customer, taking the drink order and delivering the same, relating specials, taking food orders, timing of food preparations, timing with regard to sequence of service (so that no course will ever overlap another and no course will ever be served more than five minutes after the previous course has been cleared), taking dessert and after dinner drink orders, presentation of the check, correct credit card procedures, and making correct change. This also includes the appearance of all food served, cleanliness and orderliness of the table, and, in general, the overall success of service to the customer. Proper coordination and communication with your busser and food runner is essential, since, as a server, you are in charge of giving direction to your busser. It will be helpful for you to be aware of the priorities of his/ her responsibilities. Organization is imperative.

Food Runner:

The food runner expedites customer food orders, making sure the are properly prepared, complete, and ready for delivery to all guests at a given table in a timely manner. Make sure the food presentation is correct before leaving the kitchen. Check to make sure that you are delivering the proper order to the proper guest. It is your responsibility to know the location of all table numbers and seat positions.

Busser:

The main function of a busser is to clean and reset tables, and serve bread, water, coffee, and tea. The server will direct the busser with priorities and communicate with them to ensure his/her efficiency. With proper guidance, the busser should help with cleaning plates, keeping the table clean, and providing invaluable aid to other areas of servicing the table.

Busser opening duties include:

- Making coffee and iced tea
    - Iced tea: Check the quality of what is already made and make new if needed. Restock tea bags for brewing. Keep the brewing pot, storage pot, and serving pots clean and full. Inform management if stock is low.*
    - Coffee: Clean the machine regularly as indicated by the manufacturer. Restock filters, coffee, decaf, pots, etc., and keep the area clean and stocked with creamers, and sweeteners. Milk; Half & Half; even Chocolate syrup.*
- Setting up bus carts/tubs on each side of kitchen
- Cutting lemons
- Filling ice bins
    - Ice: Clean, stocked, and scoops readily available.*
- Stocking bread
    - Bread Service: Area clean and fully stocked with napkins, plates, baskets, and serving tongs.*
    - Bread: Fresh and ready.*
    - Butter: Clean and serving dishes stocked.*
- Folding napkins for bread baskets
- Restocking linen
- Polishing silverware and glassware as needed
    - Cracker Trays: Refilled and cleaned.*
    - Salt and Pepper: Refilled and cleaned.*
    - Sugar Dishes: Refilled and cleaned.*
    - Napkins: Cloth, paper, and cocktail stocked with backup.*
    - Computer Paper/Credit Card Paper: Stocked with backup.*
    - To Go: Restock and organize (boxes/bags/sauce cups).*
    - Salad: Is it fresh or is it brown? You have the right to refuse service to any ugly salad.*
    - Salad Extras: Bacon, Onions, Croutons, Tomatoes, etc..*
    - Dressings: Fresh, clean, correctly labeled.*
    - Containers: Fresh, clean, full with proper ladles.*

Setting Up Your Station

All servers are expected to know all table numbers and different station delineations. Before setting up your station, know who your busser is and review your expectations with them. Once at your station, check the following:

- Make sure your table and chairs are clean, and that seats are free of stains or crumbs. Chairs should be straight with the table. Clean and dust all the chairs, tops, sides, underneath the seats, and the legs. Check for broken or weak chairs and report to management.*
- If Chairs are needed, take them from around the outside walls rather than from tables that are already set up.
- Make sure ice buckets are clean and ready for use.
- Napkins should be folded neatly, and centered on each place setting.
- Check your silverware to make sure it is properly arranged and that surfaces are absolutely spotless.
- Make sure glassware is polished and properly arranged.
- Make sure sugars, salt, and peppershakers are filled to the top and wiped clean. Sugar caddy should contain sugar, Equal, and Sweet & Low. Caddy should be full but not so packed that it is difficult to get the envelopes out.
- Check the floor in your station to make sure it was swept and that any dried spots or spills have been wiped up. In a word, the floor must be spotless.
  - o Floors: Make sure to check the entrances to the bathrooms. Do not assume that the least paid employee is doing their job better than you do yours. During the workday or night, make a habit of looking down. There is always something down there for you to pick-up!*
  - o Clean all surfaces: Shelves and cabinets. Restock and use proper spray cleaners and towels for the surfaces you clean.*
  - o Laundry: Clean and dirty do not belong together. Both should be maintained from start to end of shift. Do not waste but do not compromise health for thrift.*
  - o Trash: Line the containers and make sure the containers are washed and free of odors. Check regularly for trash levels and empty as needed. Do not put the trash containers near food preparation or service areas or anywhere silverware might fall into them.*

If you have any questions regarding the proper set-up and cleanliness of your stations, ask your manager.

YOU ARE RESPONSIBLE FOR THE OVERALL APPEARANCE OF YOU STATION!

Servers Opening Side Work

AM SHIFT:

1. Check the entire dining room, making sure that everything on the table is very clean and set properly.
2. Steam and buff glasses and silverware as needed.
3. Fold napkins as needed; you should have a supply of 100. A simple fold is best.
4. Stock computer stations with extra paper rolls and ribbon.
5. Wipe clean all cruvinet cards and wine lists.
6. Place flower vases on center of tables.

PM SHIFT:

1. Make sure dining room is properly set and clean, including large party tables reserved early to avoid moving tables during business hours.
2. Make sure that all sugar caddies, salt, and peppershakers are filled and cleaned.
3. Make sure all glasses and silverware are clean, polished, and properly set, stocked, and matching on each table.*
4. Fold enough napkins so that you always have a supply of 100. A simple fold is best.

Take pride in your work! This is an element of care and concern.
Don't just do the minimum; take pride in a job well done!

A word on teamwork: COVER EACH OTHER! If you are getting buried, ASK FOR HELP! Everyone will need help at one time or another, whether it is when serving our guests or doing side work. It all evens out.

Pick things up—Return them to their proper place.
Don't be sloppy, pick up after yourself and each other!!!

Phone Etiquette

Attention Maitre D', Host /Hostess, ET AL.

Don't let the telephone intimidate you. The guest in front of you is all-important and takes priority over any calls coming in after they have presented themselves for seating. If no one is available to cover the phone, let it ring until you return. You wouldn't stop to answer the phone if you were seating the Queen of England, would you?

If you're on the phone when guests arrive, conclude the call as quickly as possible and then attend to your arrivals. Never let a guest experience anything but the most professional demeanor and courtesy as they await your attention. Certainly, guests should never hear a personal conversation, or telephone rudeness of any kind.

Everyone on the floor, from owners and managers on down, should know how to answer the telephone properly.

It's: "Good Evening . . . Piero;s Restaurant. (Pause) This is John. How may I help you?"

If you must transfer the call, ask who is calling, and be careful not to disconnect the customer. If you must take a message, get the customer's full name (ask for correct spelling), repeat the phone number back to the guest to make sure it is right, and ask the nature of the call. There should be a pen and pad at every phone outlet, and all phone messages should be written out and complete. Employees with poor English skills should be advised to not answer the phone.

Greeting Guest—"Welcome!"

When greeting your guests, the all-time, absolute No. 1 customer relations' rule is: <u>Call your guests by name</u>! Do it, do it often, and do it right (doctors prefer to be called Dr., and some women prefer Ms. to Mrs.). Nothing will please them more, and guess what happens when your guests are pleased?

Host/Hostess:

The hostess is the first person with whom the customer comes into contact. You must wear professional business attire whenever on duty. Casual attire is not allowed. The hostess offers the first and the last impression of the restaurant, and is in the position to offer the kind of recognition and reassurance that will help make regular customers for the restaurant.

When greeting customers in person, say: "Welcome to Piero's—I am (*your name*), may I help you?" The hostess should try to call customers by name and be able to smooth over any delays in seating or interruption in service. If you do not know the guests name, address them as "Sir" or "Madam."

Servers:

Greet your customers with "Welcome!" This is the first thing you do when customers are seated. Even if you are busy and can't do anything else, acknowledge their presence. Within the first two minutes a party is seated, you must at least stop by and tell them you will be with them shortly. This is a must!!! As you first approach the table, let cheerfulness shine through as you introduce yourself. SMILE! Address guests as "Sir" or "Madam." Notify the manager of any "VIP" guests that you may be serving. Always stand up straight. Do not lean on chairs, tables, or booths.

When You Assume

In a resort area, when taking reservations, make a note if guest is a visitor or local. Use a V (for visitor), including hotel name, and an L (for local) on your reservation sheet, and pass this on to the appropriate parties when guests arrive. Locals will love being acknowledged (so very *in*, don't you know) and visitors will be very impressed that you know their hotel and that they are your guests from out of town. And after all, isn't that what you're being paid for?

And Yet Another Note On Assuming

A couple is not always husband and wife, so it might be Mr. Smith, yet not Mrs. Smith. Be careful in this area and only go with what you know for sure. Assuming any relationship could prove embarrassing.

Seating Guests

Again, maitre d', host/hostess (or anyone seating guests): Take your time. Invite everyone at the table to enjoy their dinner, lunch, or whatever (look 'em in the eye and SMILE) and offer the menus *individually*. The wine list should be offered after the orders are taken. Never just plop menus down and walk off. Treat your guests the way you would like to be treated if you were in the finest restaurant in the world.

One of the primary jobs of the hostess id to seat the restaurant and to do so in an equitable manner. This means that the dining room should be filed by seating each station with approximately the same number of people.

Taking & Serving Orders

When it looks like your party is ready, approach the table and describe the specials in an appetizing manner. Never recommend anything or offer any suggestions regarding any particular dish, unless, of course, management requests you do so. You will just be asking for it—trouble, that is.

If you *are* asked, assure your guests that they will undoubtedly enjoy whatever they select. If pushed into giving your suggestions, rely on that old standby: "I'd rather not recommend anything in particular since we all have different tastes. However, the chef's signature dishes are blah, blah, and blah." Or, "The special of the house is blah, blah, blah."

Once they have made their selections (never use the word "choice"), heartily endorse them after the fact. "An excellent selection, Dr. Green." You may even want to give an affirmative nod, accompanied by a pleased and pleasant smile for all to see.

And NEVER auction off the service, i.e., "who has the steak well done?" Unless you have a perfect memory, avoid this very unprofessional approach by writing down the chairs by number before taking the orders and then filling in the order for each chair. Be creative and be professional. When you input the order in the computer, be sure to have the right table number and the proper guest number, it is essential that every item be entered on the ticket. Kitchen personnel will not process any order unless it has been entered into the computer.

Once you have mastered the skills and the language, and developed the proper attitude, waiting becomes performance. So, sing with your heart, and dance with your every movement. It's show time and every shift becomes opening night!

NOTE: Do not leave your guest unattended. Stay in view of the guests as much as possible. Always check the tables in your station to determine if there is anything you might be able to get your guests. Once again, this is an element of organization.

As part of your training, you must be totally certain of cooking times for ordering any given item from the menu. If an order is not accurately timed you will be wasting valuable minutes that could be spent on the floor. It also bogs down the kitchen for others who are timing their orders to avoid overlapping. This is an important time to mention that management expects no course to overlap. **This is a cardinal sin!** Also, make sure that no course is served more than five minutes after the previous course has been cleared, unless the guest request a delay. Needless to say, poor timing also creates extra work and unnecessarily irritates the kitchen staff, which is cooking under a great deal of pressure.

NOTE ON TIMING: We will repeat it again because it is important. NEVER LET ONE COURSE OVERLAP ANOTHER! In others words, do not serve the salad when the soup is still being consumed, etc.. Always wait until everyone in the party is through with a particular course before serving the next one. For example: do not serve soup until everyone is through with the appetizer (unless otherwise requested by the customer). Never remove a plate until everyone at the table is finished with that particular course. Example: Do not serve entrees until the salad plates and forks have been removed. You may go ahead and remove a plate, however, only if a customer obviously wishes the plate removed by pushing it aside, or he simply asks you to do so.

Approximately two or three minutes after the food is served, check to make sure everyone is enjoying their meal and that nothing else is needed. Correct any problems immediately. If you cannot correct the problem, notify your manager. This is a good time to suggest more cocktails or more wine and to clear away all empty cocktail and wine glasses.

Remove the salt and peppershakers at the end of the meal when you crumb the table. This is a continual effort. Don't wait for the busser to do this. You are responsible for your station. The busser's primary responsibility is to clear and reset the tables after the customers have left and to bring bread and pate' to the tables.

When you can see that the customers are almost ready for their food, call it from the food runner. You are responsible for coordinating your entire order along with the food runner. When serving food and drinks, be careful to keep your finger away from the rims of glasses and plates. Do your best to keep food and beverages sanitary and your hands clean. Make sure that the proper order gets delivered to the right guest.

IF YOU ARE NOT PROUD OF AN ORDER, DO NOT SERVE IT.

It is the responsibility of the kitchen to prepare and serve the food to very high standards. KNOW HOW EACH DISH IS TO APPEAR AND BE PRESENTED WITH GARNISH. If you are in doubt of an order, notify the chef or manager. Once you leave the kitchen with an order, it becomes your responsibility. Protect the restaurant's reputation for quality.

Make sure that the table has all the necessary silverware for the upcoming course. Also, make sure that any condiment items that the guest may need are on the table or brought to the table with the food delivery. The guest should not have to ask for these items. THIS IS VERY IMPORTANT!

Busser priorities while serving customers are as follows:

- Make coffee and iced tea.
- Fill creamers.
- Cut lemons for the coffee/tea station.
- Serve water (tap, Panna, Pellagrino) as soon as guests are seated.
- Serve bread and pate' to the table (butter or oil upon request).
- Remove plates from the table after everyone has finished with a particular course. When clearing the table, always separate the china, glassware, and flatware to avoid breakage. Dishes should be stacked according to shape and size to allow for more room on the tray or bus pan. Do not stack more than 3 or 4 plates high. Do not hold plates against your chest.
- Assist food server with refilling coffee cups, coffee pots, and water. The guest should never have to ask for more. As you are passing by other tables, look to see if other guests need refills. This makes for excellent customer service.
- Check to see (by asking customer) if more bread is needed.
- Ensure that all condiments (cream, sugar) and service supplies (lemons, teaspoons, cups, saucers) are readily available.
- Be available at all times for guests' special requests.
- Scraping crumbs from the table.
- Vacuum the carpet in your area s needed throughout your shift.
- Once the guest has departed, promptly reset the table. Tables must be reset the same way every time so that the dining room has a uniform look. Settings are to be placed as shown to you during training.
- Maintain general cleanliness of your station.

Serving Techniques

Some Standard Procedures

When possible, *serve* at the guest's right-hand side with your right hand; *remove* from the guest's left-hand side with your left hand.
Tip for remembering: **Right-Leave the food just RIGHT. Left-remove what's LEFT.**

Set up solids (bread, salad, etc.) on guest's left, and liquids (water, wine, etc.) on guest's right. Avoid reaching across and in front of a guest to serve another guest. Do not "conveniently" serve two guests (one on either side) from the same serving position. Move to the correct position for serving each guest.

When serving a large group, keep extra silver and napkins handy. Someone is going to drop something, or use all the wrong eating utensils, guaranteed.

How Is Everything?

Timing is Everything

It is appropriate to inquire once (and not every 37 seconds) shortly after the entrées are served:

"Is everything to your satisfaction, Ms. Jones?" Stop and ask sincerely, not on the run, or as and afterthought. Look your guests in the eye to assure yourself that everything is, in fact, to their satisfaction.

You're going to learn to love doing this, and because of your excellent service and critical eye, the answer will always be "Yes! Everything is perfect!" Oh happy day!

Clearing the Table

At the End of the Entrée—"May I Clear?"

When it is time to clear the main course (you should wait until everyone at the table has finished, unless a customer has deliberately pushed his/her plate aside), take everything off the table except working drinks. Salt and peppershakers, condiments and bread should never be left on the table. Clear dirty dishes putting silverware on top, so plates will stack more evenly and not slide around. **Do not stack more than 3 or 4 plates on your arm.** Dishes should not be held against your chest. Remove all empty wine glasses. When dropping off dirty dishes in the kitchen, adhere to these rules: glassware is to be placed in the appropriate racks; plates are left on the stainless steel counter along with goosenecks; and all silverware is to be placed in the tub. NO EXCEPTIONS! If there is a wine bucket on the table, take it away. Throw away the wine bottle. Place soiled napkins in the linen bag. Put empty breadbaskets next to the bread warmer.

After you have cleared the table, ask the customers if they'd care for coffee, espresso, cappuccino, dessert and/or an after dinner drink. Do not ask your busser to take any coffee and desert orders. Make sure the coffee and desserts get charged to the customer. When serving coffee or desserts, do not place the spoon or fork on the plate. Before the plate has been set down in front of the customer, place it on the correct side. If customers seem to be lingering over coffee and dessert, you might want to ask them if they would care for an after dinner drink.

The food server is responsible to replace the silverware for the up coming courses. For example: the spoon should be on the table before the food runner delivers the soup.

To Remove or Not To Remove—That is the Question

In a more formal setting, all plates per course are removed at the same time. In a more casual setting, and only after you have asked for and gotten permission, you may remove individual plates during the meal. For a couple, however, remove plates at the same time. Use your good judgment.

Stacking

Try to avoid stacking when removing plates, especially with the slippery silverware left in between. Keep an eye on your busser in this regard.

If you can manage it, use a tray to carry everything to or away from the table in one trip. If you can't manage it, get help or make another trip.

Presenting the Check

At the End of the Meal

At lunch, when most (but not all) customers are in a hurry, present the check while they're having their coffee and/or dessert. At dinner, say nothing when presenting the check, and do not present it until the guest has either asked for it, or has declined the coffee and dessert. Do NOT ask the busser to present the check. Bussers are not permitted to handle cash or process charges.

I don't know how many times I have been presented with a check when I was looking forward to coffee and dessert. In such cases, when the guest has to ask (for dessert and/ or coffee), the waiter takes the check back, of course, but the "damage" is done. The guest is left feeling rushed. Not good. Phrases such as "Take your time," or "No rush," are completely out of line and should never be used. Silence is golden at this time.

Correct Change is Your Responsibility

It is your responsibility to see that each guest receives the correct change. It is also your responsibility to see that the correct change is in the appropriate denominations.

Example: Dinner is $30 and the guest gives you $40 (two twenties). How should the change be broken down?

Solution: All ones, or a five and five ones, NEVER a ten and two fives.

I once received a $10 bill back on such a guest check situation. Since I had planned to tip 20% ($6.00), I called the inappropriate change to the waiter's attention. He mumbled something about a new cashier, which I didn't need to hear, taking a *blame-someone-else* attitude and looking pitiful at best. He took my $10 bill and returned with a five and five ones. I then tipped 12% and vowed never to return.

About Gratuities

Better known as "Tips"

(**T**o **I**nsure **P**rompt **S**ervice)

Please note: Tips should NEVER determine the quality of service.

The Situation: You have a repeat guest who never tips. NEVER dish such a guest with other staff members, and always give him or her the exact same excellent service you give to your high-tipping guests. This is the sign of a true professional.

Some people just *don't, can't* or *won't* tip, and that has to be okay. Complaining and whining about it is not going to change it. It doesn't make such a guest a bad person, so accept it and move on in good cheer. It all balances out in the end and you'll have what you deserve at the end of you shift.

Bussers should not pick up tips from the table. Leave tip on the table for the server to pick up.

Checking Out

Before checking out, make sure all of your side work is completed. NO ONE is to leave the restaurant without permission of the manager on duty. Anyone doing so will be subject to disciplinary action. Before signing off at the end of your shift, you must have prior approval by the manager on duty.

When you are ready to check out, follow these check out procedures:

1. Separate Credit Card Tickets, Cash Checks, Guest Comps, Manager Meals, Discounted Checks, and Gift Certificates Redeemed.
2. Credit Card Checks — Staple the guest signature ticket to the back of the payment receipt. The top receipt copy will have the printed subtotal, charge tip, tax, and payment. Paperclip all of the credit card checks together.

3. Cash checks—Staple all cash checks together.
4. Guest Comps—Make sure a manager has signed each comp. Paperclip all comp checks together.
5. Manager Meals—Make sure a manager signs for his/her meal. Paperclip all manager meal checks together.
6. Discounts—If the check is an employee discount, the employee name and manager's signature must be on the check. Employee discounts ate 50% when on duty and 25% when off duty. If an employee pays with a credit card, put the check with discounts, not credit cards. Paperclip all discounts together.
7. Gift Certificates Redeemed—Staple the gift certificate to the back of the payment receipt. Paperclip all gift certificates together.
8. Duplicate/Voided Checks—If you have a duplicate check, staple the voided check to the back of the check that was paid. The check should then be grouped with the tender group (cash, credit card, etc.). If the check was just voided, paperclip all voids together.

Put your end of shift report on top of all the above and put neatly into an envelope. If there is "cash due" at the bottom of the shift report, that amount of cash must be in the envelope. Round up or down to the next dollar. For example, if the cash due amount is $100.50, the amount in the envelope should be $101.00. If the amount is $100.49, the amount in the envelope should be $100.00. On the front of the envelope write your name, total sales amount, lunch or dinner, and the amount of cash in the envelope. A manager will verify your envelope at the end of your shift.

Closing duties include:

- Making sure the hostess podium is neat and clean.
- If another hostess is relieving you, pass on any information you may have for the day.

Serving Closing Side Work:

1. Wipe clean and fill saltshakers, peppershakers, and sugar caddies.
2. Restock garridon, silverware, and plates.
3. Wipe clean check presenters.
4. Clean computer station and back kitchen station.
5. Fold napkins: 50 pre server.
6. Remove flower vases from tables—fill with water if needed.
7. Return any chairs borrowed to their place. Place chairs along the walls; do not stack them.

Busser closing duties:

- Wipe down all condiment containers, the bread warmer, the cutting boards, and bus pans.
- Restock the linen as needed.

Remove/empty dirty lien bags, combine them together, and place them outside in linen cart.

---

*With thanks to Daniel N. Griesgraber.

Offering Cocktails

If your customers already have cocktails with them when they are seated, ask them if they would like to wait a few minutes before ordering. Ask them if they would like tap water or bottled water. If bottled water, ask if they would like Panna (regular water) of Pellagrino (sparkling water). If you have customers whom you believe are under the drinking age, do not suggest cocktails or wine. If you have any doubt that they are under age, CHECK IDENTIFICATION! When in doubt, CARD! You are responsible. The penalty to you and the restaurant for serving minors is severe. If, as in most cases, the party does not already have cocktails, offer a before-dinner cocktail or wine. Direct your beverage question to the table in general, not to individuals. A very important part of your job is the offering of a cocktail before the start of a meal. Take a positive approach in your salesmanship. Treat your customers you would a guest at your home.

When taking the order, stand up. Do not lean on the table, chair, or booth. Never touch the customer. Take the women's order first. Do not leave the table until you are positive that you have taken the order correctly. If there is any doubt, repeat the order. (This is an element of your organization. Consolidate your efforts). Go to the bar and obtain drinks. You are responsible for all items delivered to the table; make sure they are entered on the check.

If your party does not want cocktails, ask them if they would care to order wine. If they do, be sure to ask if they would like their wine right away or would like to wait for their main course. Make sure you check the list (a copy of which you should jot down and carry with you) before confirming the re-order. Champagne is always served in special fluted champagne glasses. All full bottles of white wine and champagne should have an ice bucket, if available.

Note: When serving champagne, it is not necessary to offer a taste. Champagne is tasted at the winery before the final bottling takes place and airtight cork prevents it from going bad.

To save time and embarrassment, always get the necessary details at the time of order. *Example*: "On the rocks, sir?"; "Would you care for a glass with your beer, Mr. Jones?"

Important: Identify each person's position at the table from which you are taking the order to prevent having to ask, "Who gets the Martini?"

A Word of Caution

When serving those tall, top-heavy fancy drinks in the flute-style glasses, NEVER try to serve off the tray. Sit the tray down, or have someone (not a guest) help you. Actually, it makes it more festive if someone does help you, but if you're alone, and there is more than one drink on the tray, you're more than likely going to have that second drink end up where you don't want it while attempting to serve drink #1. Save yourself a lot of grief and think this out.

And NEVER serve from a *bare* silver tray or the words "slip-sliding away" will have new meaning for you. Always use a *flat* (no bumps) tray liner, or a *slightly* damp cloth.

I had my singularly worse incident in all my years of serving by not obeying the above rules. As I attempted to serve one of the three tall drinks on my tray, I leaned slightly forward, pitching the other two drinks into the lap of a very prominent food critic. I was *told* to get help, but being such a "smarty," I thought I could handle it. Well, I was wrong, and was sent home, lucky to still have a job.

The Whys and Wherefores of Wine

If there is a separate wine list, please do not assume the guest wants to see it. Ask, and then proceed accordingly. If the guests decline the wine list, which should still be in your hand, then a friendly and warm, "Very good, Mr. Clark. Your captain (or waiter) will be with you in a moment," is the appropriate response.

NEVER pour or serve drinks, especially wine, unless you know how. It takes time to learn the proper techniques. Avoid looking the fool, and do not be afraid to ask for help. We all started out not knowing about such things.

NEVER pour anything without first asking permission, not even water. "May I?" So simple, yet so effective.

NEVER have your busser serve alcoholic beverages from the bar.

When you bring wine to the table, show the label to the customer and make sure he/ she acknowledges it. If you have the feeling that the customer has ordered incorrectly, or is confused, mention the name of the wine as you present it, i.e., "This is 97 Silver Oak Alexander Valley"

When opening the wine bottle, it should be either placed on the table or hand held (but not against the body). Try to avoid "popping" the cork. After the bottle is opened, offer a sample to the person who ordered it. Once they approve, serve the women first, starting from the taster's right. If the customer rejects the wine, bring it to the manager on duty for a decision. Once the wine has been served, return periodically to refill the glasses.

Learn Your Wine

As we mentioned earlier, learn the stemware; take the time to do your homework.

Seek the wise counsel and advice of a willing sommelier (wine steward).

At the very least, learn the difference between red, white, and blush (other than their colors of course!). It will all pay off in the long run, and in more ways than you might expect. (See *Bibliography*)

Tips On The Tipsy

NEVER serve someone who is obviously intoxicated. Use the tried-and-true: "Please forgive me, Ms. Jones . . . I cannot serve you at this time. House rules." By all means get help from the management if required. You may be saving Ms. Jones' life, and saving your employer from a lawsuit, to boot.

Offering Coffee and Tea

(See *Offering Cocktails*)
Again, get the necessary details. "Do you take lemon with your tea, Mr. Smith?" "Cream and sugar, Mrs. Brown?" Getting it right the first time saves a trip or two.

Special Occasions in Serving

When There Are Children

Ignore them. Never touch them, and only speak to the little darlings as necessary, no matter how tempting it may be. In this day and age, many parents are concerned about strangers and their children. So play it safe, and stick to the above.

Also, children are real scene-stealers, and this is *your* show. You're the star of this production. Your have been warned.

Serving Friends and Family

The workplace is just that and not a place to visit and chat with friends and family. Give them the same wonderful service you are giving all your other guests and nothing more. They'll understand and admire you for this most professional stance, guaranteed.

P.S.—Obviously, this is the exception to the rule of "No first names." Of course brother Bill is "Bill," an good friend Frank is "Frank." And Mom is always "Mom." I knew you could adjust to this.

"Huggy-Kissy"

In consideration of your other guests, try not to be overly huggy-kissy with old friends, long-time customers, and/or family, unless, of course, it's your mother, or you're huggy-kissy with all your guests. Be equal in your attention, be it old friends or new friends. It's only fair.

Now, if they are huggy-kissy with you first, accept it graciously, and then move on.

Serving Large Parties

Check with the host or hostess of the group: Do they want "ladies first" service, or the more formal "serve to the right of the hostess" where the guest of honor, if there is one, would be seated—continuing on with the hostess being served last? If the hostess is also the guest of honor, then, and only then, would she be served first.

If there is a host *and* hostess, again the hostess is served *last*, and the host is served second to last. In other words, if not "ladies first," and there is a host and hostess, sitting at opposite ends of the table from each other, which is the correct seating for a formal sit-down dinner, then you would serve to the hostess's right until you reach the host.

At this point, stop, do not serve the host at this time, and begin again, at the hostess's left, and serve until you once more reach the host. Now you may serve the host. Finally, return and serve the hostess.

If the host is also the guest of honor, serve him first, wherever he is sitting.

Practice this procedure mentally at an empty table for 10 or so, visualizing the hostess at the head of the table and the host at the foot of the table, facing each other. You'll get the idea. However, if somewhere along the line, the host of hostess blurts out "Where's mine?" go immediately to Plan B, and without further ado or comment, serve them as quickly as possible with a standard, "Please forgive me"—unflustered and with a smile.

If the host and hostess are sitting side by side, the above still applies; i.e., serve to their right until you arrive back to them; *then* serve the host (second to last), and then the hostess, who is last.

If there is both a host and hostess, always defer to the hostess, unless directed otherwise, or it will be very obvious the host is running the show. Always adjust accordingly. These days, the host usually handles the bill, etc.. However, deferring to the hostess is the more formal procedure. You may never get to experience this formal service. Too bad, it was all very grand; but at least mow you have the knowledge of how it was.

The Lonely-Heart

Be on the alert of Mr. or Ms. Lonely-heart, sitting solo and probably feeling a little sorry for themselves. Be kind, be gentle, be loving, and be brief. Remember, they may ask, but they really don't want to hear about you. They really want *you* to hear about *them*. So be patient, and as attentive as time will allow, keeping in mind that someday you may be the one sitting alone in that chair.

You might want to use any influence you have to assure that those Lonely-hearts don't get stuck with that awful table halfway into the kitchen, just past the service stand. You can save that one for the couple in the shorts, wearing shower clogs, and matching plastic fanny packs. You know the ones.

A NOTE TO ALL CONCERNED (Management, Maitre d', Host/Hostess, Captain, Waiters, and Bussers) RE: THE LONE DINER . . .

It is very rude, insulting, and inappropriate to use the term, "*Just* one?" The correct and only appropriate term is "*Party of one*, Mr. Knight?" You would not say "*Just* a party of 15?" would you?

Work Well With Others

Take Care When Dealing with Others

Be aware of ethnic and religious differences, preferences, and customs, and not just regarding food. Pointing your finger at a member of your dinner party, for example, would be considered taboo in many cultures. And addressing a woman directly, instead of going through her husband, can be offensive to others. You'll learn, as you go along, and, as always, don't be afraid to ask.

Dealing With the Boss

Don't argue with your manager, you aren't going to win; nor should you. That's why your manager is called "the boss." The best route to the boss's *heart*, and every boss does have one, is through a sincere approach for help. In other words, ask your manager to help you with *whatever* the problem is, even if it is one involving "the boss."

If you have a manager or supervisor who constantly berates you, raises his or her voice at you, scolds you, corrects you, or in any way humiliates you in front of guests or fellow staff members, you may want to start looking for a position elsewhere. Your days are probably numbered anyway.

Unless it is a real emergency, never accept a personal call at work. Handle any personal calls on break, or at the end of the shift. And use a pay phone, or your own cell phone, please.

Unusual Situations

Even if you follow all of the instructions in this manual, unusual situations may occasionally arise. The following are a list of the more common situations you may encounter and how to deal with them.

REMEMBER: Rule #1. Never argue with a customer! Get the manager, explain the situation, and let him/her work things out if you have a problem.

- Food Sent Back
  If a customer sends back an item other than for reheating, get the manager to check the item first, and then have the manager go with you to the kitchen to have things straightened out. Do not throw the item away until the chef has seen it.
- Complaints About Food (but not sent back)

- If a customer complains about something but does not want to send it back, notify the manager. Some adjustments will be made.
- Wine Sent Back
  Notify the manager.
- Drinks Sent Back
  Bring the drink back to the bartender and explain the situation. Notify the manager if this becomes a regular occurrence.
- Mistaken Orders
  If a customer claims he/she ordered something other than what you brought, do not argue get what he/she wants! (If the order was taken carefully and you repeated the order where you are going. Excessive breakage through carelessness is grounds for disciplinary action.

Accidents/Spilling/Etc.

If you drop of spill something on a customer, or accidentally knock someone over (it happens), your first consideration should be the customer's well being. If you spill something, get a damp cloth and let the customer wipe them self off. Never touch the customer, unless it is to remove something that has fallen. Notify the manager as soon as possible. He/she will make any adjustments regarding cleaning costs, insurance, etc.. Avoid discussing who was at fault. Above all, tend to matters quietly and discreetly with as little commotion or disturbance as possible.

General Information, Rules, and Policies*

Below is a suggested outline of company policies and procedures that would apply to all employees. You would also receive additional information specific to your job classification. These are all excellent examples.

Time Clock

1. All hourly employees must be clocked in when they are working. In order to be paid for the correct number of hours every week, you must clock in and clock out in the MICROS system each day you work. *This is you responsibility*. Failure to clock in or out will result in disciplinary action.
2. Employees can clock in no more than 10 minutes prior to their scheduled start time.
3. All early-outs for employees must have a Manager's approval. *No Exceptions!*

Employee Meals & Breaks

1. Employees will receive a 50% discount on their meals while on duty. You will also receive a 25% discount when you (and up to three guests) dine in the restaurant while off duty.
2. At times management may prepare special meals, which will be provided to the employees at no charge.
3. Employee meals are to be consumed in Back of the House areas only, usually in the area that is not visible to the guest, unless the Restaurant is closed to the public. Exceptions will be made if all the non-visible space is in use. Employees are expected to clean up after themselves.
4. Employees will receive a paid 15—minute break after four hours of word. If an employee is scheduled to work 8 or more hours, they will receive a 30 minute lunch break (not paid). The employee must clock out for their lunch break.

Punctuality & Attendance

If an employee is unable to work, he/she must advise a *manager* at least two (2) hours prior to the start of the shift to allow the manager time to make adjustments for the absence.

Excessive absenteeism will be dealt with in a fair and consistent manner. When an employee's attendance record exceeds 6 absences in a 12 month period and/or displays a pattern of absenteeism, it will be considered "excessive absenteeism." The 12-month period starts from time of first absence. Each incident will stay on an employee's record for one year.

If the employee's absence continues for more than one day, it is his/her responsibility to call each day so that the supervisor has a clear understanding about the probable date of return. A letter from a doctor will be required if the employee is absent for medical reasons for 3 consecutive days, or if the employee shows a pattern of excessive absenteeism. The policy for attendance and punctuality will be enforced as follows:

Third incident	Written coaching
Fourth incident	Written warning
Fifth incident	Final written warning
Sixth incident	Three-day suspension
Seventh incident	Separation from employment

An attendance and punctuality calendar for each staff member will be maintained. Punctuality will be handled on the same fair and consistent manner as attendance, but will be separate when considering corrective action. Excessive tardiness is a separate offense and will be handled suing appropriate action.

A "No Call No show" is considered a voluntary separation from employment. An employee may be reinstated with a verifiable, reasonable excuse as to why they could not adhere to the call procedure.]

Appearance

It is essential that all employees be well groomed in order to present a neat, clean, and professional appearance to customers. Hair must be clean, neat, and groomed. Extreme hairstyles are not allowed. For males, your face must be clean-shaven, unless you wear a beard, in which case it must be kept trimmed. Your overall appearance must be neat, clean, and fresh. If an employee is dressed inappropriately, he/she will be sent home to change into suitable attire. A smile is part is your uniform and is required whenever serving the public.

*Special note on appearance and demeanor: Please, do not play with your hair, keep your hands out of your pockets, and dress appropriately and professionally. Leave expensive jewelry at home. For the ladies—do not wear tight clothes and watch that cleavage. Remember, you're working, not looking for a date!

Uniforms:

1. Uniforms must be neat, clean, and in good repair, free of wrinkles.
2. Slacks are required for Front of the House employees.
3. Shoes are to be black, non-skid type. Stockings or socks are to be worn at all times—free of runs, holes, etc..
4. Jewelry and make-up is to be conservative. While on duty, you cannot wear earrings of any kind anywhere except in the earlobes. This includes the nose, mouth, cheek, eyes, belly button, tongue, and any other part of your body that is visible to customers. No excessive dangles. Males may wear non-dangle type earrings only.
5. Non-uniform personnel are to dress in a business-like fashion.
6. Tattoos must be covered. (Arms, neck, hand, legs, and any other place on the body that the guest can see.)
7. Uniforms are provided for most classifications. It is the employees' responsibility to clean and maintain their uniforms. The uniforms must be returned upon separation with the company prior to your receiving your final paycheck. There will be a $150 charge for each uniform not returned in usable condition.

Behavior

1. Courtesy is a must at all times.
2. Do not socialize with co-workers, friends, or customers while on duty, unless it is directly related to your job.

3. Using, possessing, or selling alcoholic beverages or illegal drugs during work hours are prohibited.
4. Subscribe to a drug-free work environment. All employees are subject to reasonable cause drug testing.
5. Smoking is prohibited while on duty unless on lunch or breaks. Smoking while on lunch or breaks is allowed outside only.
6. Theft, in any instance, will be cause for immediate termination.
7. Violating any rules/policies or not complying with your Job Description, at the judgment and discretion of management, will result in the issuance of a Coaching Document. Upon a second offense, there will be a written warning. Upon a third offense, there will be a final warning with a suspension. If there is a fourth offense, it is cause for immediate termination.
8. Employees are not allowed to make personal calls while on duty unless approved by a manager. This includes the use of company phones and personal cell phones. You are allowed to use your cell phone while on break, however cell phones are to be locked up while punched in.

Safety

Safety is everyone's responsibility. The management staff is committed to providing a safe working environment for all of our employees. Employees are expected to obey safety rules, follow safe work practices, and exercise caution in all their work activities. If you see a spill, wipe it up to avoid a slip hazard for you your co—workers. Report any unsafe condition to your manager immediately.

Cash Variances

Any cash discrepancy, whether it is overage or shortage, needs to be brought to the attention of your manager immediately.

1. Shortage(s) over $10 in one day or $25 in two weeks will result in a verbal warning.
2. The second offense will result in a written warning with restitution.
3. The third offense will result in a final written warning with restitution.
4. The fourth offense will result in separation from employment with restitution.
5. A shortage of $50 or more in one day will result in suspension, pending investigation and/or could result in termination of employment with restitution.

Vacation/Days Off

The following procedures for vacations and days off requests will give all of the staff the opportunity to plan in advance for their personal needs.

1. Any day off request must be turned in 7 days in advance of the week you are requesting time off.
2. All vacations must be submitted 14 days in advance of the week you are requesting vacation.
3. If you call in sick on a day you requested off, but was denied, you must provide a doctor's slip or some type of documentation that helps confirm this was an unavoidable absence. Attendance policy will still apply.

We will approve or disapprove the vacation request within 5 days from the receipt of your request. It is your responsibility to check with your manager to make sure it was approved.

We will always take requests for emergency time off under consideration at any time.

Schedules/Payday

1. Management assigns schedules in the interest of providing excellent customer service while maintaining prudent cost control. Schedules are posted on Fridays prior to next week starting. Days off can be altered at the discretion of management. No days off are permanent or guaranteed. It is your responsibility to check your schedule and be at your assigned station on time. Your manager must approve any schedule changes.
2. There will be staff meetings periodically as announced by management.

Unauthorized Discounts

1. Except when expressly authorized by the General Manager, it is forbidden to give any person or cause any person to receive Company property, including but not limited to food or beverage, without proper charge or payment.
2. It is likewise forbidden to accept aforementioned company property or products without proper charge or payment.
3. Disciplinary action for this offense will be of a severe nature and handled on a case-by-case basis.
4. The only exception to this rule are that employees are permitted to consume coffee, tea, or soda in non-public areas.

General Information

1. It is the responsibility of each employee to provide his/her own supplies that are required to do their job (writing utensils, crumber, corkscrew, etc.).
2. Random checks will be made by management.
3. All employees are required to cooperate and assist co-workers if the need arises. Teamwork is essential to a successful operation. In case of any problem, discuss it in private with your manager.
4. Communication is very important in any organization. If you have a question, problem, concern, or suggestion, discuss it with your manager. If you do not get an answer from your manager, or wish to pursue a higher authority, you may discuss your issue with the general manager.
5. General and specific information will be posted on your department bulletin board. It is you responsibility to check the board daily for new postings.
6. Non-bar employees are not permitted behind the bar at any time, except when authorized by management.
7. Intentionally damaging, breaking, or abusing company property will result in termination. Excessive accidental damages will result in disciplinary action.
8. Lost & Found items should be turned in to the manager. A cabinet is in the general manager's office for these items.

A breach or violation of certain rules may also constitute a crime. An arrest or conviction for a criminal offense is not necessary to validate or justify discipline, including discharge, for a violation of employee rules.

When a question is raised regarding the meaning or application of any employment rule or any other policy or procedure, management may discuss it with the employee, but management retains the right to make the final determination as to the meaning or application of the rule.

The foregoing rules are illustrative and not exhaustive. Management has the right to determine whether particular conduct, which may not be described on these rules, is not in the best interest of the company or its operations and therefore warrants disciplinary action or separation from employment. Management has the sole right to determine the type of discipline, if any. In addition, whether the particular conduct contradicts any of these rules or not will be determined solely by management.

Thank you and welcome to the team

After reading the above rules and policies, employee must sign the attached signature sheet and return to the Administration Office. By signing you are acknowledging that you have received this manual, understand its contents, and will adhere to the rules and policies it contains.

General information, Rules, & Policies Signature Sheet

(To be removed from the manual, signed by employee, and turned in to the Administration office to be kept in the employee's personnel file.)

I have received copy of Rules & Policies and understand its contents.

Employee Name_____

Employee Signature_____Date_____

Hiring Manager_____Date_____

_____

*With thanks to Nick Tomasello.

Moving On

You have just given, for whatever reason, your two-weeks notice (and *always* give a two-weeks notice).

You now have three choices:

1. Continue on just doing your job for the next two weeks.
2. Be a total jerk and goof off for the next two weeks.
3. Really shine and do an outstanding job in the final two weeks.

Which of these three choices will make you feel good about yourself, leave your superior wishing you weren't leaving, and set up the best possible references? Your choice should be easy, but you would be surprised how many people foolishly choose number 1 or 2.

Which would you rather have said about you, as a reference: "He was an outstanding employee."
Or "I'm sorry, I could not recommend him for rehire."

It's up to you . . . it's YOUR future.

Final notes and Comments

NEVER, ever, argue with your guests. Excuse yourself if and when you feel an argument coming on; walk calmly and with composure toward your manager, and apprise him or her of the situation.

Never raise your voice or give any indication that all is not well. And don't wait until the situation gets out of hand; let your manager nip it in the bud.

Should you ignore the above and find you're in over your head, you let yourself get too emotional or out of control, you really *must* get management involved. After all, that's what they're paid for.

Always ignore any sexual comments, innuendos, propositions, or advances. If guest persists, go to management. This is sexual harassment; you don't have to put up with it, and it's against the law.

Epilogue

There are always exceptions to the rules; let common sense prevail.

Easy does it and let it flow from your heart. Let it go if you're hurt, angry, or upset. Go lovingly through your shift and you will shine like the star you are. Have fun, be kind, and enjoy what you do, as you do it. Give it your best and you'll be just fine.

Remember, not everyone is cut out to be a professional waiter. Most people don't have the talent for it.

If you find that being a waiter is not for you, get out and go back to school. Get into something steady, like real estate or acting.

Appendix I

Sexual Harassment Overview and Employee Rights

Sexual Harassment occurs when one employee makes continued, unwelcome sexual advances, requests for sexual favors, and other verbal or physical conduct of a sexual nature, to another employee, against his or her wishes. According to the U.S. Equal Employment Opportunity Commission (EEOC), Sexual Harassment occurs "when submission to or rejection of this conduct explicitly or implicitly affects an individual's employment, unreasonably interferes with an individual's work performance, or creates an intimidating, hostile, or offensive work environment,"

Sexual Harassment refers to a variety of workplace offenses.

- An employee harassing another employee can be an individual of the same sex. Sexual Harassment is a gender-neutral violation.
- The harasser can be the employee's supervisor, manager, customer, co-worker, supplier, peer, or vendor.
- The direct recipient of harassment is not the only employee who is affected. An employee who observes or learns about harassment in the workplace may file a Sexual Harassment complaint.

If you experience these or related forms of Sexual Harassment as an employee, you have the following rights.

- Tell the person or persons who are responsible for the harassment to stop doing so.
- If the harassment does not stop. Immediately bring the matter to the attention of your manager.
- If the harassment comes form a manager, immediately bring the matter to the attention of one of the managing members.

What You Can Expect From Your Employer

- Immediate investigation of the allegation.
- Protection from potential retaliation, whether it is from the person accused of harassment or any other employee.
- Protection of the rights of those employees who report they are being harassed and the rights of those being accused of harassment.
- Investigations handled discreetly, confidentially, and thoroughly.
- Appropriate corrective action according to findings.
- Documentation of each case retained in permanent files.

If you have subjected to sexual harassment or any other intimidating or hostile act while working, notify your manager immediately.

A breach or violation of certain rules may also constitute a crime. An arrest or conviction for a criminal offense is not necessary to validate or justify discipline, including discharge, for a violation of employee rules.

When a question is raised regarding the meaning or application of any employment rule or any other policy or procedure, management may discuss it with the employee, but management retains the right to make the final determination as to the meaning or application of the rule.

The foregoing rules are illustrative and not exhaustive. Management has the right to determine whether particular conduct, which may not be described in these rules, is not in the best interest of the company or its operations and therefore warrants disciplinary action or separation from employment. Management has the sole right to determine the type of discipline, if any. In addition, whether the particular conduct contradicts any of these rules or not will be determined solely be management.

After reading the above rules and policies, employee must sign the attached signature sheet and return to the Administration Office. By signing you are acknowledging that you have received this sexual harassment material, understand its contents, and will adhere to the rules and policies it contains.

Sexual Harassment Signature Sheet

(To be removed from the manual, signed by employee, and turned in to the Administration office to be kept in the employee's personnel file.)

I have received copy of Sexual Harassment Overview and Employee Rights and understand its contents.

Employee Name_____

Employee Signature_____Date_____

Hiring Manager_____Date_____

Appendix II

Saving a Life

There may be times you'll be called upon, or simply take it upon yourself, to go above and beyond the call of duty. At such times, you, and your guest or co-worker, will be glad you know CPR, insufflation (rescue breathing), or the Heimlich maneuver.

When Someone Needs Help Immediately

Insufflation (Rescue Breathing)

1. Always check if air passage is blocked. If so, clear immediately by striking victim sharply on back, between shoulder blades; or dislodge the obstruction, which may be something he ate, or his tongue, with your fingers. While you are doing this:
2. Send someone to call 911 and check if there's a doctor in the house.
3. Check for consciousness. Tap victim and shout to see of victim responds.
4. Look, listen, and feel for breathing for about 5 seconds.
5. If victim is not breathing, or you can't tell, position victim on floor on back, while supporting head and neck with one hand.
6. Tilt victim's head back and lift chin so that the lower teeth are higher than the upper teeth. This will help open victim's airway. A folded-up coat or jacket, placed beneath the victim's *shoulders*, will help maintain this position. Again, look, listen, and feel for any signs of breathing now that the airway is open.
7. If still not breathing, place your mouth completely over victim's mouth and give 2 slow breaths.
8. Check for pulse (5-8 seconds), and repeat rescue breath.
9. If still no breath, recheck position of victim's head (#6 above) and repeat numbers 7 and 8 until professional help arrives.

CPR: Cardiopulmonary Resuscitation (Heart and Breathing Rescue Technique)

1. Make sure victim is unconscious by tapping his chest, shouting, gently shaking his shoulders.
2. Tell someone to call 911 and check if there's a doctor in the house. Note: Be sure the actual address of the restaurant, and the phone number, is clearly posted on every phone for ease in giving that information when calling for help.
3. Position the victim for CPR, flat on his/her back, on floor.
4. Open the airway by placing one palm on victim's forehead, and lifting chin with other hand until teeth are almost together, but mouth is left slightly open. This may be all that's needed for the person to resume breathing. Note: If there is a neck injury, do not tilt head back; move the tongue out of the airway with your fingers.
5. Check for breathing. Look, listen, and feel; place your cheek next to victim's mouth and nose. If no sign of breathing after several seconds, repeat #4 above, checking for any obstruction, such as a piece of food, a slipped denture, etc..
6. Mouth-to-mouth: Pinch victim's nostrils together; take a deep breath, and place your open mouth completely over victim's mouth. Exhale forcefully into victim's mouth. Repeat 4 times.
7. Check for pulse at side of neck, between Adam's apple and neck muscle, for about 5 to 10 seconds. If no pulse . . .
8. Begin chest compressions: Kneel to victim, midway between shoulder and waist. Place your "weaker" hand on chest, palm pads over tip of the breastbone, with stronger hand on top, for better compressions. Lock elbows and bear down, pushing in 1.5 to 2 inches, and releasing, 5 times, to the count of 1 and 2 and 3 and 4 and 5. You should complete five compressions in about five seconds.
9. Do 15 compressions in a row, counting to 5, three times.
10. Reposition the head as in #4 above, pinch the nostrils, and again give two strong breaths, mouth-to-mouth.
11. Resume the position for chest compressions; give 15 more.
12. After 4 cycles of compressions and breathing (one set each of breathing and compressions equal one cycle), check for pulse and breathing. If neither has returned, resume the CPR. If help does not arrive promptly, see if someone else can take over for a short while.

Baby Modifications

1. Use table, or your lap, instead of floor.
2. Do everything much more gently. Necks are fragile; breaths should be puffs.
3. Place your mouth over baby's nose *and* mouth together. After each puff, be sure chest is rising. If not, airway needs to be cleared with modified Heimlich maneuver or modified blow between shoulder blades.
4. Check for pulse in baby's armpit, inside of the upper arm.

5. If a pulse, but no breathing, continue puffs at the rate of one every three seconds.
6. If no pulse, you must add compressions. Position the middle three fingers of your free hand (other is supporting baby's head) in the middle of the chest, just below nipples (feel for breastbone). Compress chest .5 to 1 inch, depending on the size of baby, almost twice as fast as on adults. Do 5 compressions (in about 3 seconds) to every 1 breath: 1 and 2 and 3 and 4 and 5 and puff.

Universal Signals of Distress

- Clutching at throat
- Being unable to speak
- Turning blue in a matter of minutes
- Losing consciousness

The Heimlich Maneuver
(First Aid for Choking, Adult/Child over 1)

1. Ask victim if he can talk or cough. If yes, he may want to clear throat without your help. However, stand by in case the situation worsens.
2. If victim cannot answer, this is a life-threatening situation. Someone should dial 911 and check to see if there is a doctor in the house while you advise victim you are going to help, with his permission.
    1. Never poke at anything lodged in victim's throat. You may end up making matters worse by forcing the object deeper into the throat.
    2. Have victim stand, and position yourself behind him. Grab victim around waist, just under the rib cage. Make a fist with one hand, thumb and fingers facing abdomen, and grasp fist hand at wrist with other hand.
    3. Keeping elbows out, press fist with a quick thrusting motion, inward and upward. This thrust is intended to clear the victim's airway by forcing air up and out the windpipe, dislodging the obstruction.
    4. Repeat Maneuver until throat is clear. If the victim loses consciousness, you can continue by kneeling over the face-up victim, with a modified thrust, or turning the victim to side and striking sharply between shoulder blades. If obstruction is dislodged, but the victim has no pulse, start CPR.

"Get Thee to a Librariee"

Bibliography

Beverage and food services. Culinary Institute of America.

Gold, C. & Wolfman, P. (2000). *The perfect setting.* New York: Harry N Abrams.

Post, E. L. & wink, L. (2000). *The wine guide.* Time-Life Books.

Wine Service. Culinary Institute of America.

Zraly, K. (2006). *Windows on the world complete wine course.* Sterling.

Online

Have a question or two on wine?

E-mail F. Paul Pacult at <u>PACULT@INTERPORT.NET</u>

Or write Mr. Pacult at
GOOD LIBATIONS
1301 Carolina St.
Greensboro, North Carolina 27401

He's the expert and he invites your questions.

About the Author

Larry knight has recently retired as Senior Butler, Bellagio Hotel, Las Vegas, NV.

He has done it all—progressing from busboy to dishwasher to waiter to maitre d' to management to owner to Butler-to-the-Stars.

He now offers the fruits of his 50 years' experience and his many observations along the way. For God's sake, take advantage of it!

Ask about our "Train the Trainer" program.

For a live presentation and in-depth review on this material, please contact:

"On the Town, Inc."
310 Market Street #1402
San Diego, CA 92101

E-mail: larryorenknight825@gmail.com

Let us bring it to life for you and your staff.

(See *Bibliography*)